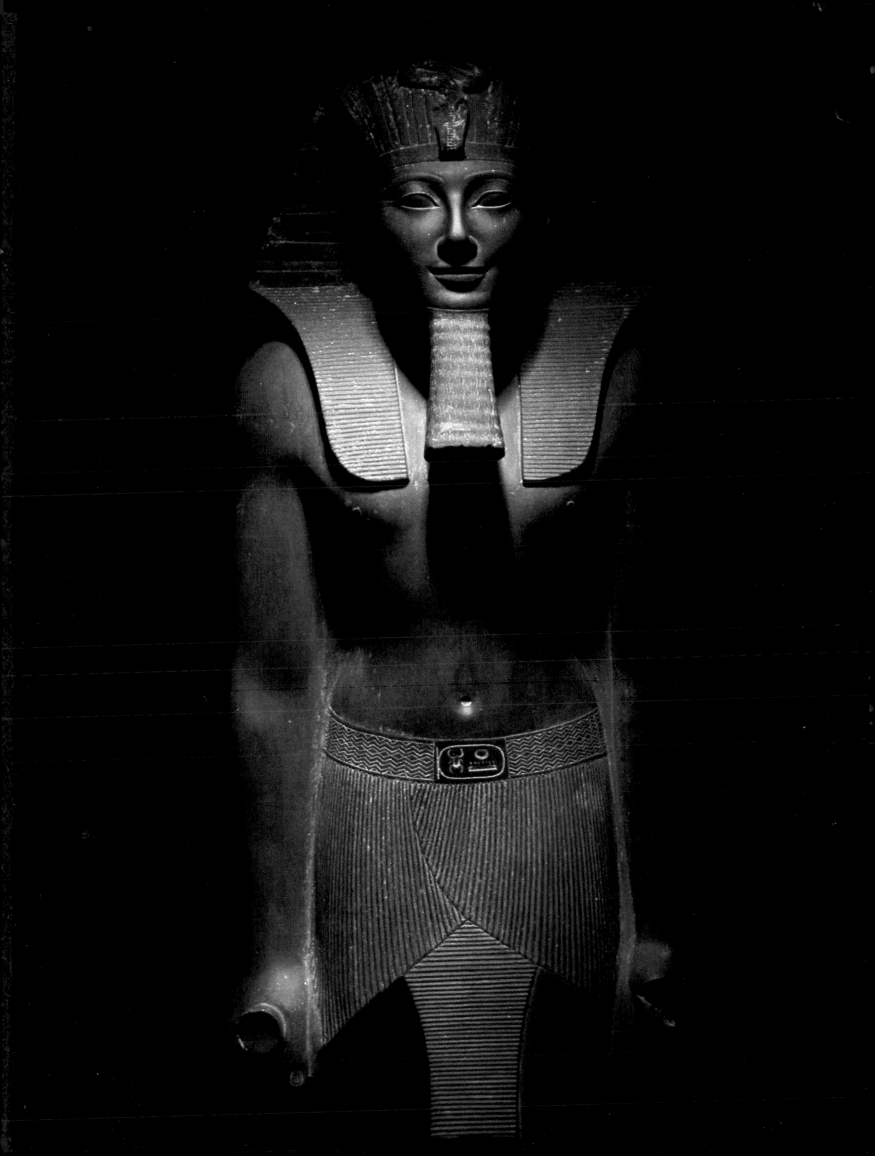

A Chanticleer Press Edition

THE EGYPT STORY

Its Art, Its Monuments, Its People, Its History

Photographs by Fred J. Maroon
Text by P. H. Newby

Consultants, Art and Egyptology: Edna R. Russmann,
The Metropolitan Museum of Art, New York
David B. O'Connor and David P. Silverman, The University Museum,
Philadelphia

André Deutsch

First published 1979 by
André Deutsch Limited
105 Great Russell Street London WC1

Prepared and produced by Chanticleer Press, Inc. New York.
Color reproductions by Nievergelt Repro, A.G., Zurich, Switzerland.
Type set by Dix Typesetting Co., Inc., Syracuse, New York.
Printed and bound by Amilcare Pizzi, S.p.A., Milan, Italy.
ISBN 0 233 97145 9

Contents

*First Frontispiece. A graywacke
statue of Thutmose III, the
soldier Pharaoh who brought
Palestine and Syria under
Egyptian control during the
New Kingdom period when the
ancient civilization of Egypt
was at its most assertive.*

*Second Frontispiece. The
architect of Queen Hatshepsut's
funerary temple at Deir el-
Bahri set it against the amphi-
theater provided by the western
escarpment. Looked at through
Western eyes, it is the finest
architectural prospect in Egypt.*

*Third Frontispiece. The best
known of various unfinished
obelisks and statues is the
red-granite obelisk in the north
quarry at Aswan, which lies only
partially prised from the rock.
This is an unfinished statue of
an Osirade figure.*

*Fourth Frontispiece. Luxor, the
site of what was once the
greatest city in the world.
Ibises, sacred to Thoth, god of
science and learning, float on
the Nile, which here may be said
to separate the great city of the
living on the east bank from the
funerary temples and tombs
on the west bank.*

*Fifth Frontispiece. The minarets
and domes of Cairo are part of
the most impressive range of
Moslem architecture in the world
— the mosque for worship, the*
madrasa *for worship and study,
the mosque tombs, particularly
of the Caliphs and Mamelukes,
and the more modest* khans, *or
merchants' storehouses, to which
caravans came from Asia and
Africa.*

*Sixth Frontispiece. The Eastern
Desert of Egypt is mountainous
and the most spectacular part of
the country. From ancient
Christian times Church Fathers
and hermits sought to serve God
by mortifying the flesh in the
most terrifying place they could
find: the desert was regarded as
the abode of demons. A Christian
there was in the front line of
the war against evil.*

Acknowledgments

No photographic effort on the scale of *The Egypt Story* is possible without the assistance, cooperation and encouragement of many individuals. To all of them I owe immense gratitude.

The good offices of the Egyptian Ambassador to the United States, His Excellency Ashraf Ghorbal, created the climate in which a book such as this could be initiated. Mohamed Hakki, of the Egyptian Embassy Press and Information Bureau, deserves a special tribute for his encouragement and involvement in all phases of the book, from conception to completion. Morsi Saad Eddin was the catalytic agent in Cairo who made all things possible. Dr. Gamal Moukhtar opened the doors to Egyptian antiquity for me. Ahmad Abushadi brought unfailing efficiency and good cheer to the project while we were photographing Upper Egypt. He, Mahmoud Ghaffar and Ehab Sherif were the long-suffering ones, who awakened with me at ungodly hours and often accompanied me until long after dark in my search for the photographic images in this book. Mona Qorashy and Happy El Gueziry generously lent me their time, support and enthusiasm, and permitted me glimpses of the private world of Cairo. My heartfelt thanks also to those here at home in America who helped make this book a reality. My wife, Suzy, helped research, edit, organize and identify the photographs, lending her practical as well as spiritual support every step along the way. Charles O. Hyman helped edit the photographs for the book's design, and the people at Chanticleer brought to the book their dedication to the highest standards in publishing. Louis Mercier, Barney Colton, Senator James Abourezk, Walter Heun, John Corris and TWA all contributed in support of various phases that made this book possible. Finally, I salute my co-author, P. H. Newby, whose heart and mind have produced the splendid text that gives so much life to *The Egypt Story.*

The Egypt Story

The Egypt Story

Introduction: Art and Egyptian Civilization

Statues of a royal prince, Rahotep, and his wife, Nofret (Dynasty IV). A high-ranking official, Rahotep was probably a son of King Snefru (c. 2600 B.C.). At this period the kings tended to restrict high office to close relatives. The superb carving is enhanced by realistic coloring and the insertion of crystal in the eyes, reminding us that statues were intended to be inhabited by the spirit of the deceased and to replace the mummies if they were destroyed. It is said that when workmen found these statues in a dim tomb chamber in 1871, they fled in terror.

When we discuss art today we tend to emphasize its aesthetic qualities and the individuality of the artist. Egyptian art is, accordingly, judged for its craftsmanship and for the visual pleasure it gives us. But these were not always the first considerations of Egyptian artists and their patrons. There was an intimate relationship between art and their fundamental belief about how to live and die. We have a quite different view. Our appreciation of Egyptian art will therefore depend on our understanding of Egyptian civilization along with our spontaneous response to beauty of design and execution.

Egyptian art is not primarily concerned with inherent beauty, but this does not mean that the Egyptians lacked aesthetic sensibilities. Their artists were gifted and they gave expression to those gifts. The royal schools of art had high standards. What they produced, particularly the more exceptional pieces, were clearly preferred to the work of provincial artists even when the latter successfully observed the standards set by the royal schools (page 20). But provincial schools also turned out clumsy work that was as aesthetically displeasing to sophisticated Egyptians as it is to us. Even within a single area and during the same period, quality and styles could vary considerably (pages 18; 28, bottom left). But Egyptian art is less concerned with beauty than with other, quite utilitarian purposes. The ancient Egyptians thought of their world as made up of opposites—desert and cultivation, plains and mountains, dark and light. These balanced each other and formed a perfect harmony. They saw the land of Egypt itself as having two elements—the Red Land, or desert, and the Black Land, or fertile areas along the Nile. There were also two political units, Upper Egypt and Lower Egypt, ruled by one king. When the land was in harmony, the Nile would bestow its yearly inundation of life-giving water. The repetition of the annual flood, generation after generation, accustomed the Egyptians to a cyclical rhythm in life. To maintain this great cycle, life had to be structured and ordered.

Being practical people the Egyptians learned early to exploit the Nile for irrigation. The strict organization necessary for such a way of life is evident in every aspect of their culture, including their art. Their art was thus governed by rules and regulations. To stray from these would mean chaotic art, and this would be against *maat*—the established order.

The Power of Tradition

For most of their history the ancient Egyptians observed a canon of proportions. A standing figure, sketched upon a limestone flake or a piece of wood or, rarely, a sheet of papyrus, would be covered by a grid: eighteen rows of squares were reserved for the figure, with a 19th for the hair. From the hairline to the neck took two rows; from the neck to the knees, ten rows; from the knees to the soles of the feet, six rows. A seated figure traditionally occupied only fifteen rows. Proportions such as these were used fairly consistently until the XXVIth Dynasty, the Saite Period (664-525 B.C.), when the rows for standing figures were increased to twenty-one and a half. After a squared drawing was finished, the grids were drawn in large scale on the walls of temples or tombs or on stone tablets (stelae) and the corresponding parts could then be sketched on the new surface. This method has been used by artists throughout the ages and is called cartooning. During the Saite Period the process was sometimes reversed. The artists of this period, using earlier compositions as models, would set up a grid on a wall from a previous period, transfer the representation on a small scale to a limestone flake, and then set it in a new location.

Right. The funerary god Osiris depicted in the tomb of Sennedjem (page 28, top left; Dynasty XIX). As king of the underworld, Osiris is commonly shown in tombs of this period as he prepares to receive the dead. While bearing royal regalia (crown, flail, and scepter), Osiris is himself depicted in mummy wrappings.

Above. Tutankhamun wearing the White Crown of Upper Egypt, in gilded wood. Some details of the figure are in gilded bronze or in glass. The figure was one of several found in Tutankhamun's tomb. The feminine proportions of the body suggest the figure was originally part of the funerary equipment of Nefertiti.

of what went on in the buildings or of aspects of an individual's life. They were meant to guarantee that everything represented would, in a supernatural and also in a "real" sense, survive forever. A man's mummified body might by mischance be destroyed but his likeness and hence his personality, repeated over and over again in hard stone or wood, would endure. A funerary cult might die out or a temple fall into neglect, but the representation of the ritual ensured that it would survive in the supernatural realm. After the carving and painting were completed, the temples and tombs were subject to a ritual which caused everything depicted in them "to live," that is, to be effective in carrying out their supernatural functions. Most Egyptian religious art—however large and imposing—was not designed for a large audience of living men. Its intended viewers were the gods, the dead, and the relatively few persons permitted to enter the innermost parts of temples and funerary chapels.

In effect, each tomb or temple created both a universe and a dwelling place for the dead man or the gods. Because of the enduring materials of which it was built and the supernatural strength with which it had been ritually endowed, this universe, this house, would last forever. In Egyptian belief, the afterlife in part reproduced the earthly life (page 22, bottom), and so scenes of daily life remained not uncommon in tombs until late in the second millennium B.C. Then the emphasis shifted to the supernatural aspects of the afterlife, and walls, coffins, and other artifacts sometimes showed the horrifying dangers the dead had to avoid. As microcosms of the universe, tombs and temples frequently had yellow stars with a blue background painted on their ceilings, and royal tombs were often vaulted to represent the heavens, complete with stars, constellations, and associated gods (page 25, bottom). A deceased king is depicted passing through the twelve hours of the night and emerging —in a rebirth—with the sun god in the morning.

Statues were also placed—sometimes in large numbers—in temples and tombs. Three-dimensional images of gods appear in the temples, where they were the focus of the ritual. In the tombs, where they provided protection for the dead, they appear only in specialized forms, as statuettes and amulets. Royal statues (page 25, top right) had various functions. In funerary temples, for example, they received the offerings, but here, as well as in the gods' temples, royal statues were also manifestations of the king, and like him, they were worshipped. Sometimes royal statuary was meant to show the king's relationship with a particular deity, as in a carved wooden head of Tutankhamun on a lotus blossom (page 25, top left), in which the young king is portrayed as the sun god emerging at the dawn of a new day. Such identifications emphasized the divinity of the king, as did the statue of a god carved in a king's likeness (page 29).

Statues of commoners placed in the funerary chapels and other parts of tombs were intended as abodes for the individual's *ka,* his essential nature. The *ka,* the life-force of the deceased, was the recipient of offerings by relatives and priests. In the early part of the IVth Dynasty some tombs contained "reserve heads"—carved limestone heads of the deceased to be used in case the head of the mummy became detached from the body. According to the early funerary spells, the Pyramid Texts, such a calamity was to be avoided at all costs. Commoners' statues in the temples portrayed the deceased in an attitude of piety; he could thus worship his god for eternity and reap the benefits of his devotion.

Tombs and Temples as Documents

Although that was not the intent of the Egyptians, their art provides

Opposite. A shawabti of Tutankhamun —a substitute figure put into the tomb to perform any manual labor that might be required of the king in the afterlife. It is carved in wood, in the king's image, with gilded jewelry and insignia.

Top Left. The infant sun god, from the tomb of Tutankhamun, with his features, emerging from the blue lotus as it opened its petals at dawn. This is one of the most popular and poetic Egyptian images of creation and of the constant renewal of life when the sun rose.

Top Center. This tiny ivory statuette of Cheops (Dynasty IV), the builder of the Great Pyramid at Giza, is the only three-dimensional portrait of the king that has survived. It was found among temple ruins at Abydos in southern Egypt. The statues of Cheops which must have embellished his funerary temple at Giza either have been destroyed or are still lost.

Top Right. A solid gold pendant, just over 2" tall, showing Tutankhamun, in a crouching pose.

Above. Part of the ceiling of the tomb of Seti I (Dynasty XIX), at Thebes. Some royal tombs had elaborate representations of the night sky, which included purely mythological figures such as Nut, the sky itself, and other mythological figures which represented planets or constellations. The latter are shown here, although only one is identified; the bull and driver represent Ursa Major.

Right. The most famous tombs of a Pharaoh to have remained more or less intact until the twentieth century were those of the comparatively obscure Tutankhamun — he was about nineteen when he died. Gold was not just a malleable metal that could be beaten into near transparency. It was a noble metal because, unlike copper, it did not tarnish; it was bright forever. It was thus the inevitable material out of which to make the mummy mask for a dead Pharaoh, and Tutankhamun's is the most beautiful to come down to us.

Above. Queen Nefertiti is a famous beauty of antiquity. Her best-known portrait is the polychrome bust in Berlin. This unfinished but strikingly modern-looking head was excavated from the studio of an artist of the time. There are other portraits of her in the Amarna style where she is disconcertingly represented like her gaunt-faced husband, Akhenaton.

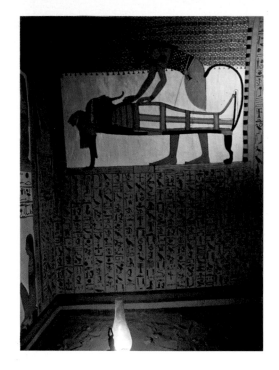

Top Left. Wall scene from the Theban tomb of Sennedjem, one of the royal artisans of Ramses II. Sennedjem's mummy is shown being prepared by Anubis, a jackal-headed god, who was the patron of mummification.
Above Left. The dwarf Seneb and his wife (Dynasty IV). This small group (13" high) is stylistically less impressive than some other art of the period, but it is cleverly composed so that Seneb's children occupy the position normally filled by the subject's legs. Seneb was head of the royal textile works and held important posts.

Top Right. Part of the funeral procession of Ramose (see pages 22, top; 71; Dynasty XVIII). The Egyptians provided not only carved or painted representations of everything the dead needed, but also the objects themselves. Here we see bearers bringing shawabti boxes, sandals, chests, a chair and a bed (the front of which, with headrest, is on the extreme left), and other objects. With a touch of humor not unusual in Egyptian art the bed carrier is being urged by his fellow (not seen here) to walk more carefully!

Above Right. Vignette from the funerary papyrus of Djetmaat- iouesankh (Dynasty XXVI). She was a "songstress of Amon," that is, a female member of the god Amon's priesthood. Here she makes offerings to Osiris, behind whom stand his wife and sister Isis and their sister Nephthys. It was Isis who reassembled and mummified the body of Osiris after it had been dismembered and scattered by his envious brother Seth. Such funerary papyri were placed in tombs as a kind of guide to the dead, for the performance of correct ritual in the afterlife.

us with much valuable information about their life and culture. Much of the information is, of course, religious. We learn about rituals (page 28, top left), burial customs (pages 28, top right; 70-71), and procedures for the afterlife (page 21). Beautifully decorated papyri give additional information (page 28, bottom right).

Scenes in temples and tombs also provide vivid glimpses of everyday life: great nobles at their duties and relaxing at banquets; artisans and farmers at work; and Egyptian and foreign troops clashing in battle. Statuettes of servants were buried with the dead. Such statues—showing servants baking, butchering, or brewing—were to serve the deceased as his household staff for eternity. Only aesthetically pleasing to us, the statues of butchers, potters, brewers, and other servants were of great practical significance to their owners. Like the carved and painted scenes on the walls, they would magically come alive in the afterlife and re-create their earthly existence.

Other servant figurines, called shawabtis (page 24), were usually far more generalized. Originally produced as substitutes for the mummy, these wooden, wax, or clay figures soon became representatives for the deceased when he was called up for forced labor in the fields of the afterlife. The statuettes, carved with the appropriate spell to answer the call, were usually placed in the tomb in large numbers, sometimes one for each day of the year. Even royalty was not exempt from this work, and royal shawabtis are not uncommon. Although rarely personalized, the figures were inscribed with the name of the deceased for purposes of identification. The shawabtis of Tutankhamun are atypical in that many of them (page 24) clearly portray the young king's facial features. Although this practice was also found in the reigns of Amenhotep III and Akhenaton, it was rarely carried to such perfection.

Any discussion of Egyptian art must mention Egyptian writing. In fact, the pictorial nature of the hieroglyphs and the narrative nature of the art makes it virtually impossible to distinguish between the two. The writing accompanying a scene (page 30) was as carefully rendered as the scene itself. The hieroglyph constituted written language, but it was also capable of artistic effect (page 31). Often, a figure in a scene will do double duty, functioning as well in an inscription nearby. This often occurs in scenes from the Old Kingdom, where the final hieroglyphic character—a seated individual—in the name of a person is omitted; the large seated figure in the scene itself serves also as a hieroglyph, thereby ending any distinctions between writing and art.

Art as Doctrine

The religious nature of Egyptian art should not obscure its social and political functions. Art and its architectural settings were addressed to the gods and the dead; but their propaganda effects upon the living were not neglected. The Pyramids (pages 82-83) impress us today primarily as bold geometric forms, but to the Egyptians they were religious symbols, representing either rays of the sun or the primeval mound from which all creation emerged. More subtly, they were also a statement of the absolute power of the monarchy. Obelisks (pages 100-101), also related to the solar cult, were inscribed with the deeds of the reigning king. The sphinx (page 33), part lion and part human, was carved out of living rock and stood, with the portrait of the king, as a guardian of the royal cemetery. Temples in later times were surrounded by fortified walls, protecting the consecrated ground from intrusion and symbolically protecting the god against supernatural enemies.

Temple reliefs of royal victories and the royal colossi in front of the temple pylons (pages 100-101) were to some degree open to the

The god Ptah of Memphis, from the tomb of Tutankhamun, a wooden statuette that is covered with gold except for eyes of inlaid glass and the blue faïence cap. Ptah was of special significance to artists, but at a deeper level, he was the god who, by the mere act of thinking and speaking, brought the world into existence. This concept exists in Christian theology, as the opening words of the Gospel of St. John indicate: "In the beginning was the word."

*Left. Hieroglyphs from a limestone
monument dedicated by King
Sesostris I (Dynasty XII). The
text gives the names and titles
of the Pharaoh. The precision
and delicacy of the carving is
characteristic of the best work
of the period.*

*Above. Scene from the mastaba
of Mereruka (page 22, bottom;
Dynasty VI). In this vignette we
see Mereruka's son Meryteti
beside his father's foot; he has
a sidelock indicating he is still a
youth. The difference in scale is
a forcible reminder that figures
in Egyptian art are scaled according
to their social importance.*

public. The people were permitted to enter the forecourts of temples and be impressed by the symbols of the prowess and power of their rulers. In conquered regions, temples had the additional role of overawing subject peoples and foreign traders and travelers. Thus the temple of Ramses II at Abu Simbel (pages 44-45) was, in a sense, an instrument of propaganda, warning the enemies of the Pharaoh of his might. Standing at the gateway to Nubia, one of Egypt's prime sources of gold, spices, ivory, and other luxury items, this "threat" was intended as a warning.

Commoners were also aware of the propaganda value of art, especially in maintaining their reputation in devotional cults for later generations. Private statues set up in temples affirmed the piety of the deceased. Some funerary stelae, having listed the virtues of the deceased, then beg the passing traveler to pour a libation before his image.

Scarabs, sacred beetles carved in hard stone, were another means by which the king could communicate with his subjects. They could as well be made of ivory, faïence, and sometimes of a precious metal. Although often functioning as amulets with an appropriate text or figure carved on the underside, they were also engraved with the king's name and issued in the thousands. Sometimes they recorded important deeds or events in the life of a king.

The individuality of the artist counted for little in ancient Egypt. A few ancient artists and architects are known today, not from their signatures on their work, but through the autobiographical inscriptions in tombs and from their names and titles in tombs and on reliefs of all kinds. The artist did not sign his work; it was not meant to glorify him or the group of craftsmen to which he belonged. It was done for the patron and was meant to glorify him alone.

Two Great Architects

The architects of two of the greatest monuments, however, are known to us. Imhotep, the creator of the Step Pyramid of Zoser (pages 88-89) was the first builder to use stone for monumental buildings. The funerary complex of this ruler, like those of all kings, had to endure for eternity, so the mortuary buildings are more or less imitations, in a long-lasting material, of standard domestic construction. Rolled-up reed mats which covered doorways are here interpreted in carved stone with insets of faïence plaques (page 35, bottom). Ceilings were made of carved limestone cylinders in imitation of wooden logs, and stone columns were fluted and topped with floral capitals to simulate bound bundles of vegetation. One of the few non-royal persons to be deified, Imhotep is referred to in later texts as the architect of this magnificent structure, and his name is found at the Step Pyramid itself. More than a thousand years after his death, he was worshipped as a god of wisdom and became the patron deity of medicine.

Such honor was not bestowed upon another important architect, Senmut, the designer of the mortuary complex of Hatshepsut (pages 2-3). He did not sign his creation, but he did have many small images of himself placed in the more remote parts of Hatshepsut's funerary temple; sometimes they were located discreetly so that the opened door would conceal the image from the viewer. Senmut was Hatshepsut's consort, so it was his relationship to the queen that concerned him, rather than the effect of his image upon others. As the queen's consort he made many enemies, and after his death most representations of him were destroyed— in Egyptian eyes, a supernatural form of execution. Hatshepsut herself fell into disfavor after her death, and much of her temple was badly damaged, though most of the great monument designed by Senmut survived and celebrates his creativity. Many of Hatshepsut's

The sphinx at Giza, a colossus carved out of the living rock and representing a recumbent lion with the features of King Chephren (Dynasty IV). In front of it (foreground) stands a stela testifying to the continuing interest of later generations; it shows Thutmose IV (Dynasty XVIII) making an offering to the sphinx and describes how the king was instructed in a dream to clear away the sand around the monument, the reward for which would be his coronation as the next pharaoh.

Above. Scene of birds from the tomb of Menna, Supervisor of Royal Fields under Thutmose IV. Menna is hunting, and on the left his hand holds two stunned birds while throwing-sticks whir among the startled birds rising from nests in the papyrus thickets. The style is loose and free, yet the essential characteristics of each bird are clear and the various types easily identifiable.

Right. A recess in the subterranean chambers underlying the Step Pyramid of King Zoser (Dynasty III) at Sakkara shows the king performing the "sed festival," a rite of renewal. The blue-and-white panels are of glazed composition (faïence) and represent the mat hangings of the royal palace.

images were defaced by order of her nephew and successor, Thutmose III, so that she would not survive in the memory of anyone. And yet apparently Thutmose himself did not want her completely forgotten. As Donald Redford puts it: "Here and there, in the dark recesses of a shrine or tomb where no plebeian eye could see, the queen's cartouche and figure were left intact. Standing alone before the image of the queen, Thutmose relented. She was, after all, his own flesh. She had not put him to death, or even deprived him of the crown. In the darkness of the crypt, in the stillness of the cells, her cold statues which never vulgar eye would again behold, still conveyed for the king the warmth and awe of a divine presence."

The Minor Arts

So far the emphasis has been on the communicative and religious nature of art. But in one area of Egyptian artistic creativity symbolism and propaganda are kept at a minimum and the aesthetic aspect is paramount. The products of the minor arts—furniture, jewelry, weapons, vessels, and so forth—had an obvious utilitarian purpose, but in some of these objects the decorative quality is just as obviously intended for aesthetic enjoyment. The Egyptians apparently liked to have beautiful things. This is especially evident in objects from the tomb of Tutankhamun. While all of these have a funerary nature, many of them were used during the king's lifetime and were put in his tomb for use in the afterlife. The furniture (page 36), chests (page 39), fans (page 38), jewelry, and all manner of other items were intended to accompany the king on his final journey.

For ordinary people, there might not be any gold overlay, inlays of semiprecious stones, or precious metals, but they could have a bronze mirror with a handle in the shape of a beautiful woman, a jar in the form of a monkey, or a cedar box with small panels of ebony inlaid with ivory. The only reason that these utilitarian objects were done so beautifully was to satisfy the taste of the designer, the patron, or both. A glazed bowl with a lovely floral scene inside it is as delightful to us as it was to the Egyptians. Even in these objects the Egyptians conveyed a message: their joy in life. To be able to produce forms of art that can exist on several levels simultaneously and be appreciated for thousands of years testifies to the enormous vitality of their art.

Ramses the Great

During his sixty-seven years as Pharaoh, Ramses II (1290-1224 B.C.) built prodigiously, raising temples, statues, and other monuments throughout Egypt. The Pharaoh was both god and man. Superhuman authority needed reiterating, so giant statues did not come singly. These two colossi representing Ramses II are in the temple at Abu Simbel in Nubia. This is the most impressive of several temples that Ramses had built in this remote southern region.

As we go into the Mummy Room of the Cairo Museum, we are already awed and confused. We have just seen such treasures as the slate palette of King Narmer, which symbolically records the achievements of the first Pharaoh over 5,000 years ago. We have seen the serene statue of Chephren, who built the Second Pyramid about 500 years later and now looks out with eyes fixed, as it might be, on some remote but certain harbor. We have seen the famous tomb furniture and treasures of Tutankhamun, which are a thousand years younger but still 3,500 years away from us. We have seen the jewelry, the graven images of gods in the form of men and animals (jackals, lions, cows, baboons, crocodiles, hawks and ibises), the models of ships and houses, the other offerings of all the thirty-one dynasties. And we have now bought our ticket and walked into the presence of the illustrious dead themselves.

Seti I, the hammer of the Hittites, the Syrians, and the Libyans around about 1300 B.C. lies here, far away from his magnificent tomb in the Valley of the Kings. There, in his sarcophagus, he lay under a blue, zodiacal ceiling. Then his mummy was removed after the ancient tomb robbers came. He is a short man with a Napoleonic chin. And here, too, is his son and successor, Ramses II, who reigned for seventy years and is the Ozymandias whom Shelley called the King of Kings. In Turin there is a black granite statue of him as a young man, looking at the same time attentive and aloof as befits the god he was. That god and warrior is now in an elaborate box. He had good teeth, a big nose, and a chin like his father's, tougher in spite of the advanced age at which he died than in the idealized figure of the Turin statue. He could now be supported effortlessly on the outstretched hands of a child.

At what point does a god and monarch become an object to be stared at as one stares at a piece of pottery or a carving? Ramses II reigned and was worshipped before the fall of Homer's Troy. Egypt was an old civilization when he was Pharaoh. But the world was so young he could not have had our sense of history or suspect that civilizations rose and fell. So he would not have been sentimental about the past as we may be. He experienced much of what his forebears had experienced. The universe did not change or evolve at today's pace.

This is not to say that Ramses II, to take him as a representative Pharaoh, lacked a sense of the past. He is actually shown on the Temple Wall at Abydos making offerings, with his father Seti I, to seventy-six of his predecessors. He would, therefore, have had a sense of chronology and sequence. He would have known that before Menes, traditionally the founder of the Egyptian monarchy in about 3100 B.C., the country was not united. He would have been aware, too, that about 1,500 years later Egypt was invaded from Asia and for 100 years or so was ruled by these aliens, the Hyksos, ("Shepherd Kings" in Greek, a mistranslation of the Egyptian for "Foreign Kings") until they were driven out. A native dynasty based in Thebes was then established which brought about prosperity. But all this did not amount to much in the way of change. Even the Hyksos invaders firmly controlled only the northern part of Egypt, the Delta, and when they had gone—possibly leaving to the Egyptians the horse and chariot—the annual inundation of the Nile came, as it always had, at the appointed season, the harvest was gathered, papyrus pith was pressed for the scribes to write on and so administer the bureaucratic society in which peasant and carpenter, embalmer and priest, all had their appointed places, their service and products at the disposal of the monarch. It was inconceivable there was any other way of living.

And dying? That was a transformation if the right kind of tomb had been built, the right grave furniture provided, and the proper preparation made for the examination before forty-two demons, ready to punish the unrighteous. If you were Pharaoh, the soul could possibly travel with the sun. There probably would be some kind of involvement in the turning of the heavens, or the rise and fall of the Nile. Today we know more clearly than ever that civilizations do indeed come and go. We also suspect that in spite of the Biblical adage a man can, by taking thought, add a cubit to his stature. At least, since the sixteenth century A.D. we have assumed that inventions will make life easier; in our wilder moments we have even thought that by reason and education man could be made free and happy. The concept of progress is a fairly modern one and was certainly unknown to the ancient Egyptians. If, in spite of the Encyclopedists, Rousseau, and the writers of the American Declaration of Independence, a certain amount of skepticism about the perfectibility of man formed in the wake of the French Revolution, there remained, and there still remains, a conviction that at least the machines will improve. Next year's model will be better. There is still enough optimism about to persuade us that change is almost a good in itself. In spite of the atomic bomb and pollution there are grounds for this optimism. The achievements of medicine alone are enough to make us believe the future will be better than the past. This psychological difference separates us from the ancient Egyptians.

It is difficult to conceive of time as a process if there is no awareness of change taking place. Ramses II, one surmises, would have regarded all those seventy-six predecessors on the throne of Egypt as living in much the same world as he did. Certainly they were dead, but their memory was alive in a way that meant they could be eradicated. The alien Hyksos rulers were left out of the Table of Abydos, and so was the heretic King Akhenaton, who upset orthodox opinion by his revolutionary monotheism. It was not unknown for a Pharaoh to have the name of a hated predecessor, like Queen Hatshepsut, obliterated from monuments. She was dead and gone, but she was still sufficiently there to be insulted and for her name to be taken out of the record.

Another difference between us and them was that the Egyptians had a kind of double vision or at least a sense that life had two parts. This sense was expressed in different ways. There was a black (of the cultivated soil) and a red (of the desert). Both aspects were real. There was life and there was death; man had a separate existence in both.

The duality of the ancient Egyptians came from the knowledge that they lived not in one country but two. The Pharaoh wore two crowns, one for Upper Egypt, where the fertile land was narrow between the deserts; and one for Lower Egypt, where the Nile branched through the Delta and villages were islands during the inundation. That was another dichotomy—time of flood and time of labor. Maybe the very peculiarities of the country set up a binary way of thinking.

Right. Ramses II is shown in his maturity in a detail from a colossal statue at Abu Simbel that now looks out over Lake Nasser. The ear of the statue is about a meter across.
Overleaf. At Abu Simbel the temple of Ramses II looked east at such an angle that the rising sun struck into the heart of it. The effect was calculated because the temple was mainly intended to honor the sun god.

Above. Nefertari was the favorite of the many wives of Ramses II. This wall painting comes from her magnificent tomb at Thebes.
Left. Ramses II fought a great battle with the Hittites at Kadesh on the Orontes, in Syria, and recorded his triumph (as in this detail of a battle) at Abu Simbel and elsewhere.
Right. The relative importance of the Pharaoh's favorite wife can be judged by the size of her statue next to her lord's foot in the Temple of Luxor.
Overleaf. In front of the great pylon, or gateway, to the Temple of Luxor there were originally six huge statues of Ramses II but only three remain.

The Pharaoh As Theologian: Akhenaton and His Predecessors

Akhenaton, the Heretic Pharaoh, has been described as the first individual in history. He was originally Amenophis IV but changed his name in honor of the Aten, the disk of the sun, the basis of his form of monotheism. The art of his time was disconcertingly realistic: nothing like this long, almost emaciated face had been seen in Egyptian royal statues before; and its like was not seen again.

Comparisons between ancient Egypt and modern totalitarian states are sometimes made, but in a way that obscures real differences. In both societies, certainly there was no freedom or respect for the individual as in Western liberal democracies. But if people are to be classified, as Isaiah Berlin has classified them, as either hedgehogs or foxes (the hedgehog knows one big truth and fits all his thinking and experience into it; the fox knows many smaller truths—experience and further thought only add to them). Former Pharaohs' names were not struck from the record for doctrinal reasons—with the one great exception of Akhenaton, who was an exceptional innovator of doctrine—but to restore what they had changed. "Render unto Caesar the things that are Caesar's and unto God the things that are God's" would have been an incomprehensible statement to the ancient Egyptians because they would have been unable to make the distinction between the truth of religious beliefs and the proper ordering of society.

One writes "religious beliefs" in the plural, for in fact—though it is dangerous to generalize over such an enormously long history—there was great variety in this polytheistic world. Different parts of the country had their ascendant gods. Sometimes, as with the Theban god Amon, their worship spread throughout the country; but it did so without detracting from the status or potency of alternative gods. The sun god Re, as the source of light and life, received homage at Heliopolis through Re-Harakhty, which means Re-Horus-of-the-Horizon, or rising sun. Justice and truth were symbolized through the goddess Maat. Death was propitiated and made less terrible through the jackal god Anubis. And so on, through all possible aspects of power and destiny, each with a cult that depended on gods in human, or sometimes animal, form. Truth was too complex to be approached through one god, and even contradictory theologies were entertained as an expression of finite human perception. The XVIIIth Dynasty Pharaoh Amenophis IV (1365-1347 B.C.) was particularly execrated because he tried to establish monotheism in a new capital at Tell el-Amarna, adopting the name Akhenaton ("effective spirit of Aten," that is, the sun disk). In the time of his successor, Tutankhamun, the priests began to restore the cult of Amon at Thebes. And Egypt resumed its traditional polytheistic, many-pathed route to the unknowable.

Halfway between Cairo and Luxor is an ancient site which provides the exception that proves the rule about the conservatism of Egyptian culture. Akhenaton built a city there on a crescent-shaped plain between the eastern hills and the Nile. After his death Akhenaton's city was only lightly populated and eventually abandoned. Here the archaeologist is therefore able to examine the detail of an ancient Egyptian city. He can study the street plan between the fourteen great stelae that still mark its boundaries and work out the site of the important buildings, in particular the royal palace and the great temple, which was two hundred yards long. It is no Pompeii. There are no remarkable buildings preserved above ground level. The interest of the site is due in part to the fact that here was enacted the first self-conscious artistic revolution of which we have record.

The excitement and indignation occasioned by avant-garde art in the modern world cannot compare with the hostility of the aftermath to the innovations of Akhenaton. Nowadays we have some realization of the link between the creative arts and the values of the society they spring from. Indignation at the "modern" movement is partly social indignation. Ancient Egyptian art, even when apparently profane,

Akhenaton adoring the god Aten, represented by the disk of the sun sending out rays tipped with hands. Akhenaton considered Aten his divine father.

had a religious purpose and innovations struck at the heart of things. Unlike the hieratic art that preceded and followed, the statues, the reliefs, and the paintings of the Amarna period are natural and realistic sometimes to the point of cruelty, particularly in the representation of the Pharaoh himself. Akhenaton, it has been said, was the first individual in history. In comparison with him earlier historical personages seem less psychologically interesting. Certainly an extraordinarily strong sense of idiosyncrasy and character comes to us down the centuries from Akhenaton. He was portrayed as warmly affectionate, sensual, and he appears to have been highly intelligent. In the huge statue of him, more than twice life size, in the Cairo Museum, he is shown with a long, emaciated face, a scraggy neck, and a fat abdomen that makes him look almost pregnant, perhaps indications of some physical abnormality. The representation is displeasing and undignified—the last effect an Egyptian sculptor would normally wish to achieve—and it must have been intended by Akhenaton himself. This repellent-looking man was married to one of the most famous beauties of the ancient world, Nefertiti, and, in one Amarna tomb relief, is shown kissing her while driving his chariot.

Akhenaton built his city where he did in part because he wanted to get away from the old religion of Thebes and devote himself to the single supreme god, Aten, which was the physical disk of the sun. His was not an anthropomorphic religion. So far as it was possible for an Egyptian to conceive of objects existing without spirit being involved, Akhenaton's type of monotheism was directed to an impersonal creative force. The great "Hymn to the Sun" engraved on the tomb of his vizier, Ay, is almost certainly composed by Akhenaton himself. It has a striking resemblance to Psalm 104 (written a thousand years later) and to St. Francis' "Hymn to Brother Sun": but it lacks their ethical fervor, though this defect may be due less to any lack of moral insight than to a lack of explicitness. "All work is put aside when you set," the poem goes. "Since the world was made, you make prosper the king, your son, who came out of your body, the king of Upper and Lower Egypt, the Lord of the Two Lands, who lives in Truth." The Egyptian word used for "Truth" was *maat*. In his poem Akhenaton lays great emphasis on the moral coherence of the universe; in the tomb reliefs the rays of the impersonal solar disk are shown coming down from heaven, but terminating in human hands holding the hieroglyph for "life." The sun becomes a hand; the hand is human, and promises that the universe is not indifferent to human destiny. The very naturalism of the art which Akhenaton encouraged was doubtless an expression of rapport with the real world. Be honest, be truthful, be natural! The universe is as it is and the propaganda of the priests of Amon will not make it different. It would be too much to read into the Tell el-Amarna remains any suggestion of democracy. Akhentaton had set up a new state religion dominated by himself, his family and the new god.

His wife, Nefertiti, is known to us from the celebrated portrait head of her now in the Berlin Museum and the unfinished head with dreaming eyes now in the Cairo Museum which was excavated from a Tell el-Amarna studio. It is a face that has the same enigmatic quality as Leonardo's Mona Lisa. In his poem Akhenaton refers to her as "the King's Great Wife, whom he loves, the Lady of the Two Lands, Nefertiti, may she live and prosper in happiness for always." What happened to her after the death of her husband we do not know. She may even have predeceased him. The priests of Thebes were strong, and may have forced the youthful Pharaoh Tutankhaten to recognize the old ideology of Amon; and he became Tutankhamun, whose tomb, by a freak of history, is the only royal tomb from the Valley of the Kings to have survived without being totally robbed in antiquity; Howard Carter found it nearly intact in 1922.

In the great temple enclosure of Karnak a stela was erected, in the name of Tutankhamun, which spoke of the misfortunes that had befallen the land during the reign of Akhenaton. From the island of Elephantine in the south to the marshes of the Delta, the temples dedicated to the gods had fallen into decay. Weeds had grown in their courtyards and peasants had used them as shortcuts from one field to the next. There is a reference to the frontiers of Egypt which gives the impression that under Akhenaton the defense of the empire had been neglected. Although it might appear that Akhenaton was an eccentric pacifist who neglected the military responsibilities of his office, there is evidence to the contrary.

In 1888 A.D. a peasant woman was digging for *sebakh* in Tell el-Amarna. This is fertilizer, the nitrogen rich debris of ancient towns. Being Nile silt, it was ideal for breaking up and spreading over the land, particularly as it often contained straw which added useful humus. But it was a good day for history because this woman uncovered a lot of clay tablets, too, and they turned out to be from the registry of Akhenaton's foreign relations department. It seems that just as in Europe from the Renaissance until the twentieth century the language of international diplomacy was French, so in the time of the New Kingdom the international language was not Egyptian but Akkadian, which was the language of lower Mesopotamia set down in cuneiform—that is, wedgelike writing on clay. These Tell el-Amarna tablets have provided firsthand evidence of the international wrangling of the time—the marriage treaties, the trade agreements, the alliances proposed—which must have been going on in much earlier times, too. It is salutary to be reminded how international relations flourished and how much the Nile Valley was in touch with the valley of the Tigris and the Euphrates. But there are letters, too, from Egyptian governors of parts of the Egyptian Empire in Asia. One, from Syria, is almost inarticulate with anxiety. "All is finished . . . give me horses, chariots, men. The enemy is marching upon us. Give me thirty companies of horse. I need men. Send men and chariots. I am without what is needed. I have not a single horse." Such a letter shows signs of exaggeration.

The neglect of the ancient gods, then, and the possible neglect of defense were enough to make the name of Akhenaton execrated. He was described as "the Enemy" after his death.

Just when the Israelites were captive in Egypt and from which Pharaoh they fled continue to be matters of learned debate. There are those who even doubt whether the Israelites as a whole people ever lived in the Land of Goshen; perhaps, they argue, there were certain tribes who came down from Canaan in time of famine and were used as slave labor by the Egyptians; and other Semitic tribes were left behind. Certainly the orthodox story is that the Jewish people as a whole were held captive in Egypt and that they made their escape under Moses. That the account in Genesis and Exodus is based on a real and terrible experience is beyond doubt and there is general agreement on where the Children of Israel were held in captivity. Precisely when this happened, we are not quite sure.

If you drive northeast of Cairo on a British-built side track, you find yourself on a desert ridgeway looking north to the Delta, which you see as a fringe of palms and a flat green wash of growing crops. Out

there is the site of the city Pi-Ramses, where the Pharaoh lived and where the state granaries for that part of Egypt were located. This is the Land of Goshen, and the Pharaoh who most fits the Biblical image was the son of Ramses II, Merenptah. He was certainly the son and successor of Ramses; and the Book of Genesis talks of Egypt as the land of Ramses, who was followed by the Pharaoh who "knew not Joseph." So much of the detailed information about Egypt given in the Old Testament squares with the knowledge that comes from using one's eyes in the Egypt of today. The making of mud bricks with straw and then putting them out to dry and harden in the sun is only the most obvious. Another is the evidence from tomb paintings of the granaries of ancient Egypt that reduced the possibility of famine and made the country an attractive place to enter if your own homeland in Palestine was suffering from drought.

On a granite stela at Thebes there is an account of Merenptah's military successes, and this refers to Israel—"Israel is desolated and has no seed"—rather as though Israel was a country. The text goes on to make a plain reference to Palestine and Syria (Khor was what this area was called) and it is hard to resist the idea that we have here a reference to the story told in the first chapter of Genesis. The Egyptians were afraid because of the high fertility rate of the Israelites. If they multiplied they might join the enemies of the Egyptians and fight against them. So Pharaoh Merenptah ordered a policy of infanticide. "Israel . . . has no seed," he boasted. This mention of Israel is the only one in Egyptian writing of the Pharaonic period and it is remarkable how it supports the Exodus story.

The Red Sea is a mistake. There was never any question of the Israelites making their escape across the Red Sea, whether by divine intervention or not. The Hebrew should properly be translated not as the Red Sea but the Sea of Reeds, and there seems little doubt that the Bitter Lakes were intended. What the configuration of land and water at this time was, there is no way of knowing, but it is easy to imagine pursuing Egyptian soldiers coming to grief in the marshes. The Israelites would naturally not take the usual road to Palestine because of the Egyptian outposts along the route; better to strike southeast into Sinai because that led nowhere except to the copper mines, which could be avoided by striking into the hinterland. If this theory is correct—and scholarly opinion is weighted in its favor—the exodus from Egypt took place in the thirteenth century B.C. (Merenptah reigned from 1224 to 1214 B.C.), which is roughly the time when Troy fell to the Achaeans and the dead Hector was dragged behind the chariot of Achilles.

When the Israelites lived in the Land of Goshen they practiced agriculture as the Egyptians did, which was very different from the farming they did in Canaan. They were accustomed to a rain-based cultivation and it must have been strange to live in a land where it rarely rained and water came from the irrigation canals. They can be imagined in the northwestern part of the Delta, where cotton is now the main crop, learning the new techniques, raising water from one level to another by *shadoof*, and then controlling the flow by building earth embankments. When the water had to be diverted from one crop to another, they would break down the little embankments, perhaps by using their feet in a way the Egyptian worker in a market garden will today. In Deuteronomy 11:10 we read: "The land which you are entering to occupy [Canaan] is not like the land of Egypt . . . where after sowing your seed you irrigate it by foot like a vegetable garden." Anyone who has seen a fellah using his feet in this way will know precisely what the writer is describing.

55

Left. This diorite statue of Khaef-Re (called King Chephren by the Greeks) came from the Valley temple of his pyramid at Giza and is now in the Cairo Museum. He built the second-largest Pyramid at Giza; another portrait of him is thought to be the face of the Giza sphinx.

Below. Thutmose III, the Napoleon of the Pharaohs, fought seventeen campaigns in twenty years. If there ever was an Egyptian empire he was the Emperor. His elaborate atef crown, combining the attributes of several gods, emphasizes his divine status. So much of the temples, tombs, arts, and other objects of the New Kingdom dynasties have come down to us that this period may seem more real than any other in Egyptian history.

Right. Pharaoh Nebhepetre Mentuhotep of the XIth Dynasty. The sandstone statue found under the courtyard of his mortuary temple at Deir el-Bahri is painted, so we know the robe is white; he wore it for a jubilee celebration after reigning thirty years. His crown, with the peak at the back, is the Red Crown of Lower Egypt.

Overleaf. To Amenophis III, husband of the famous Queen Tiye and father of the Heretic Pharaoh, Akhenaton, we owe much of the splendor of the Theban temples. His great servant and namesake, Amenophis, son of Hapu, was responsible for setting up the images of the Pharaoh known as the Colossi of Memnon.

Nefertari was the Great Wife of Ramses II and her tomb is in the Valley of the Queens, in the great Theban necropolis. Nefertari is shown here with the goddess Isis. Her mummy, with almost chestnut-colored hair, worn in ringlets, is in the Cairo Museum. The hair color may be due to mummification or the passage of time; but an original light color, though exceptional—for most Egyptian hair was black—is not impossible.

The rulers of ancient Egypt were unlike other rulers because from the earliest times right up to the Ptolemies they ruled as gods. The divinity of kings was a concept that passed from the native Pharaohs to their Ptolemaic Greek successors. In turn they transmitted it to Rome; from there in the European Middle Ages it took on a new life and, one cold January morning in London in 1649, led to the execution of Charles I. This may sound like an unwarrantable telescoping of history but there is continuity of a sort. It is most certainly a fact of ancient history that the Romans deified their Emperors after the Egyptian example and that modern Europe is the child of Rome—which is what Pascal had in mind when he wrote of Cleopatra's nose. The supreme god Re or later Amon-Re was the father of each and every Pharaoh, which is another way of saying that the Pharaohs begat children both as men and as gods. To us, the complete command of their subjects and the country's resources that this unique status of the Pharaoh implies is no doubt unattractive. Society was not only conservative; it was rigidly hierarchical and, thanks to an army of scribes and bureaucrats, efficient in its control of detail. This did not necessarily mean tyranny. There is evidence that the kingship was held in some affection. Certainly there were no popular uprisings. Although the Pharaoh was god on earth and theoretically possessed all the land, crops, and animals in his domain, the system was humanized by a general acceptance of the idea that men lived under a law of universal justice. The Egyptian word for it was *maat*, and the goddess Maat was a sedate figure, with an upright ostrich feather on her head. It is the same word that Akhenaton used for "Truth" in his "Hymn to the Sun."

The word *maat* has no precise modern equivalent. It seems to mean that the universe was good. Shakespeare would not have known the word, but a speech he put into the mouth of Ulysses (in *Troilus and Cressida*) expresses part, but only part, of what it signified.

The heavens themselves, the planets and this centre,
Observe degree, priority and place,
Insisture, course, proportion, season, form,
Office and custom, in all line of order:
And therefore is the glorious planet Sol
In noble eminence enthron'd and spher'd
Amidst the other . . .
Take but degree away, untune that string,
And, hark, what discord follows! . . .
Force should be right; or rather, right and wrong,
Between whose endless jar justice resides,
Should lose their names, and so should justice too.

A priest of Amon, unlike Shakespeare, would have thought this platitudinous. Shakespeare wrote, though, out of an experience of social and political change. The lines have a vehemence that suggests they were expressing a view not far from Shakespeare's own: the structure of society is fragile, we shall only survive if everyone knows his place in it and accepts the same scale of values. The priest would have been more complacent. Whatever departures from the norm there might be—and if he lived at the time of Ramses II he might have thought of the Hyksos invasion and the monotheistic heresy of Akhenaton—the created universe had a moral order that was as apparent through the observed forces of nature as through the relationship between the Pharaoh and his people. The priest would not have known how to distinguish between the two.

61

Right. The goddess Selket was found in Tutankhamun's tomb and is associated with the scorpion. The goddess was one of four positioned protectively around the shrine containing the king's mummified internal organs.

Above. Hathor, goddess of love and joy, had her most famous temple at Dendera, near Luxor. In this granite representation she is shown with the ears of a cow, her sacred animal, but sometimes she wears horns with the sun's disk between them, for she is a sky goddess as well.

A Different People

The ancient Egyptians were not an overtly sensual or erotic people as were people farther east in Mesopotamia and India. For long periods they even seem to have been rather decorous. Herodotus went out of his way to say that the Egyptians, unlike other people, did not allow "intercourse with women in the temples . . . the Egyptians are exceedingly strict in their reverence for holy places in this as in other ways." Herodotus was writing in the fifth century B.C.; there is general agreement that Egyptian beliefs and mores were decadent in this period, so in the Old and New Empires one can suppose even severer views. This is at variance with the popular view of behavior in the Nile Valley. It was not the view of the Romans, who, perhaps, were transferring their own somewhat priapic values to a civilization they were temperamentally incapable of understanding. Even Osiris, as fertility god, does not often reveal himself in an open sexual way. Usually he is as respectable as a bishop. The wall paintings showing girls naked or in transparent dresses are not erotic. The evidence that sex played a major part in Egyptian belief and behavior does not exist and it is impossible that they thought of obelisks—as no doubt someone has suggested—as fertility gestures. They were symbols of the sun, the main architectural feature of early sun temples, and later associated with Amon.

Women played a more important part in the political life of Egypt than in any other ancient civilization. After the death of Tutankhamun, his young widow seems to have written to the Hittite king Suppiluliumas asking him to send one of his sons to marry her. She promised that he would become Pharaoh. This implies great authority, and possibly a little desperation. At the time of making the proposal the young Ankhesnamum—for that was her name, she was the daughter of Nefertiti and Akhenaton—must have been of near-Pharaoh status herself. At least two earlier Pharaohs had actually been women, not counting the celebrated Queen Hatshepsut, who was the most formidable woman, Cleopatra not excepted, in Egyptian history. She wore the double crown, dressed as a man, and is chiefly remembered today because of the magnificent funerary temple built for her at Deir el-Bahri backed by the western cliffs of northern Thebes. The great temples and palace of Karnak on the eastern bank of the Nile embody the popular idea of Egyptian architecture—huge, highly decorated and powerful rather than elegant—but here at Deir el-Bahri are a delicacy and humanity that foreshadow the Greek. It is remarkable, not only for its dramatic position, but also for the nobility of the architecture. By walking up a central ramp the visitor would have seen successive white colonnades opening up in the brilliant light, cool against the Theban hills. Even today the porticos remain. Hatshepsut sent a trading expedition down the Red Sea to Punt and here, in the temple, it is all recorded in the reliefs, with pictures of African animals and plants and the fat wife of the local king.

Another great lady who came a little later was Akhenaton's powerful mother, Queen Tiye, for whom a large artificial lake was dug where she sailed her pleasure boat, *The Aten Gleams*. We do not know what influence she had on her son's ideas, but he formed them when very young and it is not implausible to suppose that she was determinant. She was a real power behind the throne of her husband, Amenophis III. Her daughter-in-law, Nefertiti, may well have remained in Tell el-Amarna after the death of her husband, Akhenaton, when the succeeding Pharaoh Smenkhkare returned to Thebes and the religion of his forefathers. She may have stayed in the heretic's city with the

Top, Above. Nakht was clearly rich, for he and his wife had musicians, singers, and dancers in their household who performed at banquets for guests, such as the women shown above, being waited on by a serving maid.

Above. A scene of mourning in the tomb of Ramose (pages 22, top; 28, top right). The burials of great men required an impressive funeral procession in which the women of the household were expected to express dramatically the grief suppressed by other, more restrained participants. Tears were shown streaming down the faces of the women and some throw dust over their heads; undoubtedly loud ululation would also be part of the activity.

child Tutankhamun. If so, that would imply a commitment to monotheism. But we cannot be sure about Nefertiti. She may even have died before her husband. A conversation between Queen Tiye, Akhenaton, and Nefertiti, conducted perhaps on her boat in the lake, can be imagined at an earlier period in their lives. Sweep away the complicated ancient cults and establish something more coherent, they might have agreed, as the sail filled in the night breeze and they scudded by flaring torchlight under the walls of the great brick palace. We know from their portraits in wood and stone exactly what these women looked liked—tense, quick, and nervous as thoroughbreds. Cleopatra, in beauty, intelligence, and royal power, had her precursors.

Apologists have been known to say that Christianity introduced a new respect for women by the importance it attached to the mother of Jesus. In comparison with Islam, Christianity is more explicit about the dignity of women. Under Moslem law a woman has, however, certain rights of property owning and inheritance that were unknown in Europe until recent times. In Pharaonic Egypt women were property owners and could be of such status that a mere man might become Pharaoh not because of who he was but because he had married the Pharaoh's daughter. Women had a recognized place in the running of their families. But women were powerful figures in the pantheon, too, and autocrats, on occasion, in the ordering of the state.

Wives could be shown in symbolic statuary, like that of Ramses the Great at Abu Simbel, as coming no higher than their husband's knee. But women could and indeed did rule and they had splendid tombs. There was one extraordinary moment when, in the thirteenth century A.D., a woman ruled as Sultan of Egypt. It is fair to say there was no other Moslem nation where such a state of affairs would have been tolerated, and it may have been possible because of the agreeable Egyptian tradition of feminine power. It was quite foreign to the male-chauvinist Romans, and may be another reason why Cleopatra made such a conquest over them. Freud, no doubt, could explain the charms that power can exert where only femininity had been expected.

This painting of Sennedjem, a royal artisan, from his tomb at Deir el-Medina near the Valley of the Kings, shows him and his wife harvesting in the afterlife. They are not wearing work clothes, which suggests that their activity is largely ceremonial.

Left, Above. From the tomb of Nakht (at Thebes), peasants are treading on grapes and, to maintain their balance, holding on to ropes tied to a beam. Nakht's tomb contains brilliant paintings of agricultural life — plowing, sowing, and, as shown here, packing harvested ears of grain into a basket.

Top. Menna was a land steward and estate inspector about 1400 B.C. His tomb shows the harvesting of crops — of wheat, papyrus, and date palm. In this scene, above, the crop is being measured for tax assessment, and it has been suggested that the woman, at the right, is carrying a bribe for the assessors.

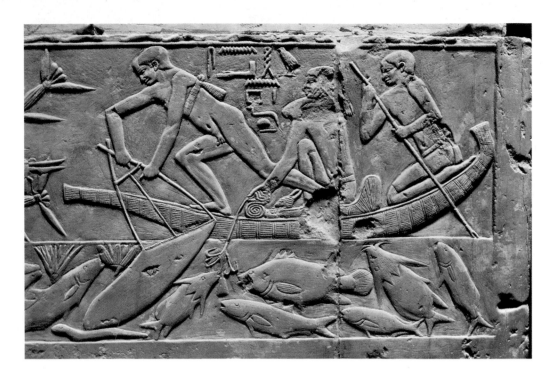

Top. This relief from the
tomb of another official at
Sakkara shows fishing from a
papyrus boat in the Delta with
a fishing line and a trawl net of
a kind sometimes still in use.

Above, Right, Overleaf.
The elegance and realism of
reliefs in the tombs of high
officials at Sakkara reflect life
in 2500 B.C. and earlier. These
views of food are from the
double tomb of Akhtehotep and
his son Ptahhotep, Vth Dynasty
dignitaries who lived in
Memphis in the valley below.
Since the game is still alive and
the grain newly harvested, these
ritualistic scenes are to assure
the dead man and his son that
there will be a perpetual food
supply in the life to come.

The Meaning of the Pyramids

Pyramid tombs were built for most of Egypt's great Pharaohs between 2700 and 1600 B.C. Later, when kings no longer used them, smaller versions were built for private tombs. Their symbolism is connected with sun worship, and it may be that the shape, a depiction in stone of the sun's rays, was thought to aid the dead king in his ascent to the heavens. The greatest of the Pyramids, those at Giza (pictured here) are among the earliest. But not even the wealth and efficiency of Egyptian society could sustain such enormous efforts indefinitely: later Pyramids were much smaller, and much more poorly constructed. Overleaf. Of the Pyramids at Giza only Chephren's retains some of its outer casing of Tura limestone at the top. It appears taller because it is on higher ground. The farthest one is the Great Pyramid of Cheops; the nearest is the Pyramid of Mycerinus.

Building a Pyramid was not quite holiday work, but anyone who has seen the humor with which present-day Egyptians work as a team (pulling a car out of a ditch, for example) might guess there was rhythmic singing, clapping, and laughter at Giza too. They labored during the annual flood when no other work was possible.

We actually know what the architect of the Great Pyramid at Giza looked like because a lifelike limestone statue of him survives. He was the cousin of Cheops (whose tomb is the Great Pyramid) and his name was Hemiunu. As represented, he could be in his forties. He is undeniably a fat man, with sagging breasts and a small, rather tight mouth. It is dangerous to generalize about people's characters from their appearance, but the impression he gives is one of considerable toughness, even ruthlessness. Notwithstanding his gangster-like presence, he might have been the jolliest of men, handing out extra rations when some particularly huge piece of masonry had been levered into position, and ready for a laugh with the astronomers when they were working out the precise alignment of the Pyramid in relation to the northern stars and the known relationship this bore to the sun in its zenith — which, with a stick in the sand, could be determined when the shadow was at its shortest. One can imagine him supervising the clearing of the foundation. It would be solid rock cut to make a perfectly level platform around the core of rock left to be at the heart of the Pyramid. Precision was achieved with the same techniques that controlled the Nile flood down in the valley; water would be enclosed by mud walls and the submerged rock face cut away until it lay at the same depth below the surface. Hemiunu would have needed massive patience to ensure that this was done properly. No doubt he was as tough as he looks. One thing he would have been certain about. He was not, as some modern theorists have supposed, incorporating all mathematical and astronomical knowledge into the structure of the Pyramid. Nor was he prescient about the future. He was building a tomb for his royal cousin and the inspiration for it may have been no more abstruse than the fact that the Pyramid structure could rise to a greater height than any other. The apex was nearer the heavens than even the apex of an obelisk. Earlier pyramids can be seen as an evolution from the simple oblong brick structures, known as mastabas (the Arabic word for mud benches), which went before. The Step Pyramid at Sakkara, which is a pleasant camel ride away from Giza to the south, suggests a staircase to the heavens. Even today, when one stands at the foot of the Great Pyramid and looks up its dilapidated flank to the remote summit, there is a sense to be gained of an aspiration to the heights. When originally built it was cased in smooth limestone. At certain times of the day this must have given off an overpowering, almost stupefying heat and brightness. Seen from the right angle and at a distance, the faces of the Pyramid would have lit up, like distant windows in the sun. Surely it must have been intended to represent the sun's rays in a way that allowed the dead king to ascend to heaven? When there are clouds the sun's rays can sometimes be seen to strike through a gap at about the same angle as the slope of the Great Pyramid. Anyone who has seen this not uncommon phenomenon will certainly be convinced that this massive tomb is a tribute to the sun.

It is, thus, a mistake to regard the Pyramids as elaborate follies built for the gratification of the king and resented as such by the hundreds of thousands of laborers who sweated over the years to build them. The work was holy. The building expressed the way ancient Egyptians understood the cosmos. The worthwhileness of such work would have

The Pyramid of Meidum was probably the burial place of King Huni but had to be completed by his son, King Snefru (c. 2600 B.C.). It was originally designed as a Step Pyramid but was finished as a true Pyramid. Its casing has collapsed or been removed revealing part of the original structure which may have been used for the mastabas built nearby.

been no more questioned than, to the Christian mind, was the building of the great cathedrals in the Middle Ages.

A short distance to the south of the Great Pyramid complex, but still on the Giza plateau, stands the Great Sphinx. It seems that when the builders of the Pyramids were quarrying stone here they left a sizable outcrop, which was fashioned, at the time of the building of the Second Pyramid, that of Chephren, into a lion with a human head. Our understanding of the Great Sphinx, and all the many other sphinxes that one finds throughout Egypt (notably the famous avenue of ram-headed sphinxes at Karnak), tends to be muddled by the Greek idea of what the beast stood for. To the Greeks she was a sinister female with wings who represented the mysterious power of death. To the Egyptians the sphinx was a lion, the traditional guardian of sacred places. Sphinxes usually had human faces and the Great Sphinx has that of Chephren. As the king was believed, after death, actually to become the sun god Harmakhis, what we have in the Great Sphinx is the symbolic representation of Chephren in his role of guardian of the Giza tombs. Perhaps "symbolic" is the wrong word. The Egyptians did not necessarily make that distinction between a representation and what was being represented. King Chephren was Harmakhis, and there he crouched, wearing the royal headdress, the cobra, and the beard, with his paws in the sand.

All the Pyramids worth seeing are within thirty miles or so of Giza. The most remarkable is the Step Pyramid at Sakkara, which was built for King Zoser by his vizier Imhotep. Imhotep was clearly a man of the most remarkable gifts, a kind of Leonardo da Vinci of the third millennium B.C., for not only did he build this, the first large stone building in the world, he was also in later tradition an astronomer, a writer, a wise man, and above all a physician who was later deified as the god of medicine, whom the Greeks called Imouthes and identified with Aesclepios.

The traveler can see the Pyramids of Giza from his hotel window in Cairo. Indeed, some of the rooms in Shepheard's Hotel were so constructed that the fortunate occupant can sit in a comfortable chair and gaze out across the Nile (which is so wide here as to look more like a lake than a river) to the Pyramids. The obvious way of improving one's acquaintance with Pyramids would therefore seem to be simply to drive out to where they are. It is much better to take a bus or taxi which should transport you through the Cairo suburbs, across the river to the Bulaq, and then south, on the west bank of the Nile to a village called Badrashein. Here there are donkeys. One sits well back on an Egyptian donkey to get the best of this means of transport. One of these elegant, pewter-colored animals will quickly convey you west into the shade of palm groves where young women in black clothes, partially veiled, and wearing a lot of colorful ornaments in their headdresses and across their breasts, may be discovered, as in Arcadia, driving or more probably leading sheep and goats. Here and there are little mounds of rubbish and rubble. There are fields of clover and perhaps watermelon. Depending on the time of year, onions or maize and bearded barley will be growing. Flies have to be driven away with a whisk. A passing camel, carrying a load of dried dung for fuel, or baskets of dates, will sigh like a tired old man, but apart from that there is silence. You are at the heart of what once was the great city of Memphis, of which nothing now remains. It was in this city the builders of the Pyramids lived.

One suspects that the first monumental Pyramid, which rises on the desert bluff to the west of where the city was, might have been something of an accident. It sounds almost impious to say so because its architect, Imhotep, was such a great man he was later regarded as a god and one does not like to say anything that detracts from deity. The fact is that there were lots of flat, benchlike tombs before Imhotep's time, and what he did in effect was to make a rectangular one, put another, smaller one on top, and so on until he had made a step Pyramid. It is still there—the oldest stone building in the world. If, instead of ascending by steps, the structure rose up in a straight line the building would mimic the way the sun's rays came out from behind a cloud. The development was inevitable. Such a structure would not so much symbolize the divine (because the Egyptians didn't know what symbols were), it would *be* divine.

Only monarchs were entitled to build Pyramids until after c. 1550 B.C., when Pyramids were not used for royal burials and commoners built small ones over their tombs. It was in order for the Pharaoh to arrange for tiny Pyramids, no more than two or three hundred feet high, for his wives. Even viziers and high priests had to be content with mastaba tombs, looking like long boxes, arranged decorously at the foot of the Pyramid as, no doubt, in life they had arranged themselves in the Pharaoh's audience chamber. Sometimes boats were constructed and buried close to a Pyramid, perhaps one on each of the four sides. At one time it was supposed that such boats were intended, in some ritual way, to serve the Pharaoh after death in his voyage across the skies or on the waters of the underworld, but so many boat pits have been found, notably at Giza, that it is now thought the Pharaoh might have needed them for a ghostly trip on the Nile, too.

On the evidence we have it seems a prosaic civilization. But we know little of its poetry and almost nothing of its music. Only its art speaks to us directly across the millennia. The most moving members of the Egyptian pantheon, Isis, Osiris, and Horus, demonstrate something of the spiritual insights possible in the Nile Valley from ancient times. But our information is limited, and we have to be prepared in our understanding of Egyptian monuments for an acceptance of the view that the people who built them thought that the nature of the universe could be understood in terms of the daily life of priests and peasants under the Egyptian sun, and what made sense to these practical people would make sense to the supreme god himself. The Pyramid, that is to say, was—having regard to the nature of the universe—the most desirable of all possible permanent abodes.

First Overleaf. Unlike the Greek Sphinx, Egyptian sphinxes did not ask puzzling questions. They were leonine images of kings who guarded holy places and the Giant Sphinx at Giza shows the builder of the second Pyramid, Chephren, as a lion. In later times he came to be regarded as a sun god.
Second Overleaf. The Step Pyramid of Zoser at Sakkara, built about 2686 B.C., is the oldest stone building in the world. The architect was Imhotep. His achievements and power were so great that he was later venerated as a god, and great wisdom, especially concerning astronomy and medicine, was attributed to him. Before Imhotep, kings had tombs with flat tops, but he designed a new type of Pyramid by stepping one mastaba, as the earlier tombs are called, on top of another.

could reach him. He was the last of the native Pharaohs. In fact he was the last native ruler of Egypt until General Naguib, well over 2,000 years later. He went south. He left the Delta and went first to Memphis, passing the cluster of great Pyramids at Giza on the way, and then disappeared even further south, beyond Thebes and its great temples, beyond the splendor of Karnak and the cataracts to Nubia, where he was heard of no more. What happened to the deep Egyptianness of the people when that flight took place and the Persians came in with fire and sword? In what sense did they use the word *maat* when their cities were plundered and their young men murdered?

That the ancient Egyptians ever had an empire in the sense that the Persians or Romans did is unlikely, but if such a spread of power existed it was centered on the great city of Thebes in the sixteenth century B.C. Thebes was then the largest and richest city in the world. Homer called it "hundred-gated Thebes" and pictured the mounted warriors riding through these gates and the pile of treasure that was to be found in its temples. This was the area from which the resistance to the invading and hated Asiatics, the Hyksos, was directed, and when it proved successful, military expeditions, particularly into Syria and Palestine, were made by the warrior Pharaohs Thutmose I and his grandson Thutmose III. The wealth of the world flowed to their capital. Tribute and gifts came from Assyria, Babylonia, from the Hittites, from Crete, and from Mycenae. The vast complexes of temples that, in ruins, one now finds at Karnak and Luxor were at the heart of this metropolis. On the other side of the Nile were funerary temples of unparalleled splendor, the rich tombs in the Valley of the Kings and the Valley of the Queens, gigantic statues, artificial lakes, palaces, and populous quarters where laborers worked in the service of funerary pomp.

The Pharaoh was possessor of all, in theory, but in practice the temples enjoyed great endowments rather as monasteries did in the Middle Ages. The great Temple of Amon at Karnak controlled in its prime a high proportion of all the landed property throughout Egypt assigned to the priests. The Pharaoh, returning in triumph from foreign conquest, would present gold, jewelry, and slaves to the god. It was his concentration of wealth and power that made possible the building of such huge edifices as the great Hypostyle Hall, with its massive papyrus columns and calyx capitals; these ponderous and highly ornate columns are so placed that, viewed from a certain angle, there seems to be no space between them. The soaring forest of stone seems impenetrable. Then, by moving a few feet, the rows seem to move apart and the light—if it is morning—strikes brilliantly from the east and the reliefs and inscriptions appear to march around the great columns and across their architraves as they have for more than three thousand years.

What we see in the great Temple of Amon is not the work of any one Pharaoh. It went on for over a thousand years, each Pharaoh seeking to emulate his predecessor with his own particular grandiloquence in stone—Thutmose I and II, the extraordinary Queen Hatshepsut, whose great funerary temple is on the other side of the Nile, Ramses I, Seti I, and Ramses II all contributed. As one walks up the avenue of recumbent rams to the great portal of the temple one is doing what the worshippers did all those centuries ago, proceeding into the Great Court and so to the Hypostyle Hall, beyond which, in a remote dark chamber, lit only by a shaft of sunlight from overhead, was the god himself. To see him was the privilege of the Pharaoh and the highest priesthood.

Except on high days and holy days. The god, then, was paraded in his sacred boat, which was really rather a grand, ritual version of the

The statue of the lion-headed Sekhmet, the goddess of war, with the light falling on it through an opening in the ceiling, is in the temple of her consort, Ptah, built at Karnak by Thutmose III.

94

barge the Pharaoh used on the Nile, and, like the Pharaoh himself, the statue, still in its shrine, would be protected from the sun by a kind of tent, kept cool by fans at the end of long poles, and followed by singing priests. But in normal times the god kept to his temple.

The energetic and prodigal Ramses II built everywhere. Some distance to the south of the Great Temple of Amon is the huge Temple of Luxor, likewise dedicated to Amon. To the range of pylons, courts, and colonnades already there Ramses II added a great court which has now, in part, been taken over by a mosque. The whole temple has suffered its changes. At one time it served as a Christian church and at all times it has been pillaged for stone to make other buildings and had houses built between the columns. The dwellings of princes, priests, and ordinary people have long since disappeared, having returned to the mud and dust out of which they were built; for it was only sacred buildings that were made of stone. If we are to imagine the splendor and vitality of this great city we must see the temples surrounded by houses, plastered white on the outside and plastered inside, too, to carry wall paintings; there would be meaner buildings for the less well off but with little courtyards where porous clay pots sweated in the shade and fruit trees grew in the neat cottage orchards. The use of money was unknown, so all transactions, from street markets to the disposal of the annual harvest, were effected by an elaborate system of barter. At night, in the summertime, people slept on their flat roofs for coolness, with rush mattings slung on poles to protect them from the light of the enormous, brilliant moon and scarcely less brilliant stars.

One of the few royal palaces that has been discovered is that of Amenhotep III. Now called Malkata, it is on the west bank quite close to an artificial harbor, the Birket Habu; the latter is distinct from another lake built near Akhmim for his wife, Queen Tiye, in 15 days, according to contemporary writings. It was built at a time when Thebes was at its most prosperous. Amenhotep III celebrated his jubilee in a special hall where all the images of the gods from the various regions of Egypt were brought together to take part in the sacred processions and dances. Of his mortuary temple all that now remains are the two huge statues of him—wrongly called the Colossi of Memnon by Romans (pages 204-205). In antiquity the northern one reputedly gave out a musical note at sunrise but it has been mute ever since the Emperor Septimius Severus repaired it. The stones were quarried at Heliopolis 400 miles away, transported, and erected by the celebrated functionary Amenhotep (son of Hapu), who was so revered he, like the wise old Imhotep who had built the Step Pyramid, was deified. His cult lasted until Roman times. But of the rest of this great temple nothing remains. The site is cultivated, as is much of what was once a city of many thousands of inhabitants behind their great walls and their hundred gates. Well, perhaps not a hundred. Homer has been known to exaggerate.

Above. The exuberant Ramses II could not restrain himself from adding an extra court in front of the existing temple at Luxor, but these papyrus-like columns are part of the colonnaded courtyard built earlier by Amenophis III.
Opposite. The Hypostyle Hall in the great Temple of Amon at Karnak is one of the greatest architectural achievements of antiquity. These huge inscribed columns are inspired by the papyrus plant. The capitals are simulated calyxes—that is, the opened sheath of leaves around the open papyrus flower cluster. The scale of this work is prodigious. These columns in the central nave are, including the capitals, about 80 feet high. In the aisles the columns are smaller and have capitals in the form of a papyrus bud. Altogether there are 134 of these warm brown sandstone columns in the Hypostyle Hall which was, in the main, built by two Pharaohs, Seti I and Ramses II.

Right. There are more architectural relics of Ramses II than of any other Pharaoh. The reliefs on the entrance pylon at Luxor celebrate his campaign against the Hittites and the battle of Kadesh. He sits, in ruined splendor, with his back to the record of what he considered his greatest military achievement.

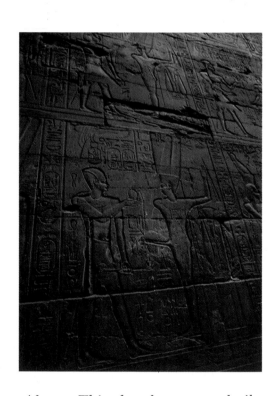

Above. This chamber was rebuilt in the time of Alexander and shows him before Amon and other gods.
Overleaf. The great entrance, or pylon, of the Temple of Luxor contained no fewer than six colossal statues of Ramses II. The obelisk was originally one of two erected for his jubilee. The other is in the Place de la Concorde in Paris.

The Greeks and Alexandria

Alexander founded the city in 331 B.C. to keep open contact with Greece and thereby protect his flank in the Asiatic campaign he was planning. He decided the plan of the city but did not stay to see any of the work done. Alexandria became a great trading center and then a cultural center that made a permanent contribution to civilization. This portrait bust is in the little Greco-Roman Museum in the city.

In less than ten years after the departure of the last native Pharaoh, Alexander arrived and was welcomed as a liberator. The Greeks had a long association with Egypt. There had been an old tradition of Greek mercenaries (and, interestingly, Jewish mercenaries, too). Greek traders and scholars had been at home in the country since about 600 B.C. But 332 B.C. was the first time that Greeks ruled Egypt. For long it had been considered by them to be the originator of their gods and their teacher in the arts and sciences. In recognition of these religious roots, Alexander went to the oasis of Siwa in the most celebrated pilgrimage of antiquity, there to be inducted as Pharaoh by the priests of the Temple of Amon.

Significant as the visit of Alexander to Siwa was for the development of ideas about monarchy, the greatest contribution he made to civilization was the founding of his city. There was an Egyptian fort on the site, Rhakotis. Why, one wonders, had it not developed? The spot was easy of access from Crete and southeastern Europe. Indeed, Homer records that Menelaus landed there on his voyage home from Troy, the first European to visit Egypt we have record of.

Anyone who goes sea bathing in Egypt will know there is a current running from west to east so strong that at certain places one returns to the beach well to the east of the point of departure, exhausted by the fight against the flow of water, which is often brown with Nile mud and running like a river. This current led to the silting up of the mouths of the Nile, but Alexandria is at a point on the coast where the current does not bring in silt. So it provided a clear harbor. Off the coast here is a line of islands, the most important of them being Pharos, where in due course the famous lighthouse was built, about 600 feet high and one of the wonders of the ancient world. Why a lighthouse of such height? It was not so much to warn shipping of rocks as to tell sailors where Alexandria was. Coming in from the north the sailor was on the Egyptian coast quite suddenly because it is so low-lying, and then, in the comparatively unmaneuverable boats of the time, had a hard slog beating along the coast with a northerly on his port or starboard. The more warning of where he was, the better. The first he would see of Egypt would be this finger sticking up, apparently out of the sea itself, an obvious landmark by day and a light at night—created we know not precisely how.

Alexander marked out the plan of the city in person, showing where the marketplace should be, and where the temples to the various gods, Greek mainly but Egyptian as well, should be located. For all the vicissitudes through which the city has gone, the street plan is much the same as Alexander wished it. One main street ran from west to east, with the Moon Gate at its western extremity and the Sun Gate at its eastern. Cutting it at right angles was another principal thoroughfare. These two streets are still there, though the classical layout of the other ancient streets is now obscured. A kind of embankment, known as the Heptastadium, was built to link the island of Pharos with the mainland. The accretion of years has made this into quite a formidable neck of land and as one now walks through this populous sector of Alexandria it is hard to realize it was once sea.

The most striking relic in the modern city is Pompey's Pillar, which is of red granite from Aswan. It has nothing to do with Pompey the Great, though for a long time it was supposed to mark his tomb. Pompey was murdered as he came ashore many miles to the east, near Pelusium in the eastern Delta, with Julius Caesar in pursuit, but the column is more ancient. It marks the site of the great temple of Alexandria, the Serapeum, and one theory is that wherever it was originally erected it was brought here and put up for the Emperor Diocletian in 297 A.D. The worship of Serapis, of which this was the center, but which later extended through the Greek and Roman world, is interesting because the Ptolemies seem to have encouraged, or even created, this artificial amalgam of deities as the basis for a state religion. The god is represented as a handsome, curly-headed athlete with a corn basket on his head. Yet he is clearly intended to incorporate some of the attributes of the Greek Pluto, god of the underworld. More important, he is also, as his name indicates, Osiris and the bull god Apis. He was very successful. At this distance of time it is hard to see just why. Perhaps it was because he expressed both strength and suffering; Osiris was the god who was murdered, brought back to life by a devoted wife, and lived to reign as King of the Dead. Those who believe Pompey's Pillar was erected to mark the triumph of Christianity over paganism fix on the date 385 A.D. This is when the temple was destroyed and the great stone god smashed. To explore the remains of the Serapeum nowadays is a dismal experience. One touches clammy limestone and walks dark passages through which the gods took flight and never came again.

Smelling salts, or sal volatile, or sal ammoniac, have gone out of fashion, but every time the word "ammonia" is used the oracle at Siwa is being invoked. Here, near the Temple of Amon, ammonium chloride was first made from the dung of camels, and it is not too outrageous to suppose that the fumes may have played some part in the operation of the Oracle. Exciting and narcotic fumes traditionally put the god or goddess into the appropriate frame of mind for the utterance of wisdom. At Delphi, the great religious center of ancient Greece, the Pythian goddess inhaled vapors which came up from a break in the rock. We can imagine the ram-headed god sweating in a dark chamber at Siwa as the pungent odor of camel dung excited his mind. There really was something special about the Oracle here because at one time the Greeks had a special trireme, called *Salaminia Ammonias*, that transported envoys to Mersa Matruh—or Paraetonium, as the Romans called it—so that they could make the long, hot, and dusty journey to put questions about whatever major problem it was they couldn't get the appropriate comment on at Delphi. This was why Alexander came to confront the god in some dark and stinking chamber, a god one must imagine in the form of a man with a ram's head. The silver tetradrachms that Alexander had struck after the Oracle had confirmed his divinity show him with great ram's horns. Maybe he wore ram's horns in real life, on state occasions, as emblematic of his divine ancestry.

The remains of the temple can be seen, but the visitor to Siwa is more likely to be struck by the beauty of the enormous palm groves and the many springs of water and small pellucid ponds where from time to time bubbles rise through the tinted water in winking clouds and then stop as though some underground blower had put his pipe aside. Herodotus mentions the Spring of the Sun, which, he said, grew hotter and hotter as the night progressed until at midnight it actually boiled. He never actually went to Siwa. The spring is still there, but the water does not boil; but then, neither does the northerly of the two Colossi of Memnon sing when the first rays of the risen sun strike this great statue as it was reputed to do in antiquity. Perhaps this Colossus did sing, perhaps the water did boil—there would be no lack of natural explanations for such phenomena—but wonders do grow in the telling.

Alexander founded his city mainly to secure control of the Mediterranean behind him while he pressed into Asia, but it became a trading

The temple at Kom Ombo overlooking the Nile was put up in the Ptolemaic period when Isis, here shown on a pillar, had become increasingly revered. She was the wife of Osiris and mother of Horus—the ancient Egyptian "holy family."

Mohammed Ali, the Albanian, is often described—and with justice—as the creator of modern Egypt. He was certainly the creator of modern Alexandria. In the course of centuries the place had sunk to insignificance. The discovery of the Cape route to India had a lot to do with its decline, but so too had the rise of Cairo, which was the inevitable political and administrative center of a country more interested in the Arab roots of Islam than in the Mediterranean. The canal linking it with the Nile silted up and by the time of Mohammed Ali in the early 19th century the population had sunk to something like 4,000. He built a new canal, the Mahmoudiya, linking the city with the Nile and established a residence in Alexandria. From his time until that of his descendant King Farouk, the court and the Egyptian government went to Alexandria for the summer months. They preferred the famous cool north wind that blew off the sea every afternoon to the heat of Cairo. The present Egyptian government continues to operate throughout the year from Cairo; and if there is a certain national pride in remaining throughout the torrid days in the national capital there is also the compensation that the nights are a lot less humid.

Alexandria occupies a place of special importance in the intellectual history of mankind and it occupies, also, a special place in the literary imagination. This white city by the blue sea is the setting for Shakespeare's *Antony and Cleopatra* and Dryden's *All for Love*. A modern poet and a modern novelist also speak for Alexandria. Constantine Cavafy was a Greek who was born and lived all his life in Alexandria (he died in 1933) except for short periods. He brings to contemporary subjects a sense of history. He was acutely aware of the Hellenic culture of which the city of Alexandria itself was the remarkable expression. But Alexandria withered, as civilization itself, Cavafy seems to say, is bound to wither. His most famous poem is "Waiting for the Barbarians." The novelist who speaks for Alexandria is Lawrence Durrell, whose *Alexandria Quartet* provides a very personal, almost *fin de siècle* view of modern Alexandria. The real subject of both Cavafy and Durrell is culture and the decadence of art.

Right. Pompey's Pillar has nothing to do with the Roman who opposed Julius Caesar in the civil war, though he was murdered at Pelusium. It was probably raised for the Emperor Diocletian (in 297 A.D.), who had put down a rebellion and, in the old Egyptian tradition, was a god. The column marks the site of the temple of Serapis, who was a peculiarly Alexandrian god, with the attributes of Osiris and Apis. His cult became widespread in the Roman world. Overleaf. Mohammed Ali, the Albanian who laid the basis for modern Egypt, constructed the Mahmoudieh Canal in 1820 to link Alexandria with the Nile and so re-establish it as a trading center after centuries of neglect.

The River Gives All

Pharaonic Egypt was the most conservative society of which we have record. It endured for a very long time. The span is roughly the same as from the great classical age of Greece, the fifth century B.C., to our own day. This extraordinarily persistent civilization took root in a fertile valley protected by seas and deserts from invasion; it was an agricultural society totally dependent on the annual flooding of the Nile. Social organization on a large scale was useful in controlling the inundation in basins and canals. This contrasted with life in mountainous countries, where clans were fiercely individualistic because the terrain was unsuited for a large, settled, highly organized society.

Blaise Pascal said three hundred years or so ago that if Cleopatra's nose had been shorter the whole history of the world would have been different. Great consequences can flow from rather minor but matter-of-fact circumstances. Whether he was right or not about Cleopatra's nose, there is one little fact about Egypt that has had the greatest consequence. The river flows from south to north and the pace of its flow is unexpectedly swift. The brown waters swirl under the arches of the Cairo bridges and boatmen have to fight against it. Were it not that the prevailing wind in Egypt is against the flow of the Nile, from north to south, there is little doubt that the unity of Egypt would have had to wait for a time later than the year 3000 B.C. With a northerly wind behind them, simple, unmaneuverable boats could put up their big rectangular sails and travel upstream—that is, south—from the Delta to Thebes and beyond, right up to the first cataract. They sailed to Aswan for granite. The return journey downstream could be made rowing with the current, sails furled. Egyptian history is usually explained in the terms Herodotus defined when he said the country was "the gift of the Nile." The black silt brought down from the Abyssinian mountains is highly fertile and a prerequisite for settled life in the country—so much so that the Egyptians called the whole country "the Black Land," or Kemi. But the opposition of wind and Nile was also crucial. It made good communication, and thus political unity, possible. The Egyptians may have been slow to use the wheel in warfare—not until the Hyksos introduced horses and chariots a thousand years after the Pyramids were built—but they were quick to exploit the physical and weather resources of their country in order to organize society on a greater scale than anywhere else. This organization made possible technical and philosophical achievements of a high order.

If we may judge by the present-day Egyptian peasant, the ancient Egyptians were a humane, humorous, unfanatical people who in their practical, down-to-earth way found it more natural to get on with each other, to share out the life-giving water by interdependent canals to the farthest possible basin of cultivation, than to go in for tribal warfare, though it would be wrong to suggest such warfare did not go on from time to time. The history of Egypt can be seen as the relationship between peaceable cultivators and the predators from desert and mountain. The stability of Egyptian society was due to the freedom, for something like the first thousand years of its history, to develop in its own way without being subject to invasion.
Egyptians—in spite of the boasts of Ramses II and other warrior Pharaohs—were only at exceptional times a military people; indeed, they made such unenthusiastic soldiers they were not allowed to enlist in the Roman legions. Yet they probably made soldiers as good as any others except when compelled to fight for a cause they did not

The Nile is the only source of water, and although great improvements have been made recently in securing a pure supply, many rural areas still get water only as the river provides it. Traditionally women have carried it, as in this scene at Kena in Upper Egypt.

support. Their relatively non-militaristic spirit was nurtured in a privileged African enclave where the human race, as a result, acquired a succession of technical skills—stonecutting, architecture, mining and smelting, metalworking, surveying, the making of writing material out of the pith of the papyrus reed, agriculture, animal husbandry, medicine—that otherwise might have been lost, or developed more slowly, in more volatile societies. And when the invaders did come, the Hyksos, the other Asiatics, the Persians, the Greeks, the Romans, the Arabs, and the Turks, the essential spirit of Egypt was not changed. But once they lost control of their own destiny in the fourth century B.C. (there was no native ruler of Egypt from that time until the revolution of 1952—that is, for almost 2500 years), they became the most exploited and misgoverned of people.

As to their beliefs, it is surprising that the Nile was never a major god, that the king was a god, and that, unlike other people, the ancient Egyptians did not unduly emphasize a link between the fertility of the land and human sexuality. They saw it but made comparatively little of it. Without the Nile, Upper Egypt—that is, southern Egypt—would be desert. The Egyptians did not know where the water came from, and in all probability in the second millennium B.C. they did not know what caused it to rise every year so dramatically. We now know it is due to summer rains in Ethiopia feeding the two major tributaries of the Nile, the Blue Nile and the Atbara. The Nile was not apparently worshipped for itself, or bathed in (as the Ganges is) as significant ritual. A crocodile god called Sobek represented the power of the Nile to rise and fertilize the land. The fertility god Osiris, too, was seen to operate through the Nile, but he was not the Nile; he was far too grand and mysterious for that.

There is a Sherlock Holmes story in which the famous detective drew attention to "the curious incident of the dog that did not bark in the night-time." In trying to pin down the special nature of Egyptian culture one ought to look to the Egyptian dog that did not bark, though the Sumerian, and the Assyrian, and the Hebrew dog did. What elements in these other Middle Eastern cultures are lacking in Egypt? One very important distinction we do find is that Egypt was unique in having a king who was also a god. But Egyptians did not worship their river as one might, in all innocence, suppose; nor did they see the relationship between sexuality and the fertility of the soil in quite such powerful terms as we find in the ancient civilizations of the Mesopotamian valley. There is nothing comparable to the Sumerian story of the Flood that we find set out, in the account of Noah and his ark, in the Book of Genesis.

The absence of a Deluge story is perhaps the easier to explain. In the Tigris-Euphrates Valley the flooding was unpredictable and led to disaster and death. In 1929 Leonard Woolley was sinking a pit in the Royal Cemetery of Ur when he came upon a deposit of mud many feet thick; below the mud he found flint implements and pottery. It was his belief that this mud was deposited during the Biblical flood and, if so, the nature of the disaster was evident. And the impression it made on the memory of mankind was evident, too. In Egypt no comparable disaster took place. Even in the Delta you can dig down sixty feet or so through the Abyssinian silt and come across no remains of any culture or civilization until you come to the bedrock. Unlike the rivers of Mesopotamia, the Nile brought fertility and prosperity to Egypt and its annual rise was a matter for rejoicing—and anxiety when it did not rise in the expected way. We cannot imagine anyone in the lower Tigris-Euphrates setting up a flood measure, as the ancient Egyptians did when they installed a Nilometer at Aswan. The Nile has never been a source of fear.

To the Egyptians the creation of the world was rather like the land emerging after the Nile flood had receded, a primeval hill rising out of the ocean of chaos. The beginning of things was explained in other ways, in stories of men being made from the tears of Re or by Ptah out of clay. In spite of the many stories, Egyptians were not as concerned with this problem as the Babylonians or the Hebrews, possibly because their attitude toward time and history was different. Being as astonishingly conservative as they were, change of any sort was only reluctantly acknowledged; so "the first time," as they called it, the supreme change from non-being to existence, was described in several creation myths.

The gathering of taxes, either in kind as in Pharaonic times, or in kind and cash as in more recent times, was—after religious observances and the making of war—a central preoccupation of all Egyptian rulers. How was the level of tax fixed? In years when there was a "poor Nile" the peasant clearly produced less. A "good Nile" made for plenty and a greater ability to pay. There is evidence that the level of taxation was related indirectly to the height of the Nile flood; taxes were calculated on anticipated yield. Praise was regularly given to rulers who were not demanding in poor years, but the system was more precise than that. From the most ancient times the level of water was calculated. Wells were sunk not far from the riverbank and at the bottom of them would be a tunnel connecting with the river. As the water in the Nile rose so it rose in the well and the rise could be read on markings either at the side of the well or on a central column. Such Nilometers are to be found, dating from about 1500 B.C., at Medinet Habu in Thebes, at Edfu and the island of Elephantine. The one at Aswan was of particular importance because, as the southernmost, it was the earliest to detect the flood. The most famous Nilometer was built by the Arabs at the southern end of the Island of Roda in Cairo in 861-62 A.D. This is an elaborate stone structure with a staircase and a central octagonal column marked in ells. When the water had risen to something more than 15 ells (or 27 feet) the signal was given for cutting the embankments of the irrigation canals, particularly the one leading into Ezbekieh, and general rejoicing broke out.

Overleaf. The Nile is low at Beni Hasan in Upper Egypt and the fellah moves at no greater speed than his ancestors three thousand years ago.

Farmers of the Black Land

Anyone who has walked in the Egyptian fields in the early afternoon will not believe the labor there is never-ending. The peasant may have risen with the sun and, sitting on his donkey, trotted out to his plot with a hoe over his shoulder; but soon after the sun has reached its zenith and the shadows are shortest he is to be found stretched out in the shade of a palm tree or under a mud wall with a rag over his face, perhaps, to protect him from the flies. Sleep has always been the shortest way out of a sometimes intolerable existence. Yet it would be a great mistake to suppose that, even under the Turks, his mentality was that of a slave.

Pasha was the title of the Turkish administrator who ran the country under the twenty-four Mameluke princes. The title continued right up to the present. Only thirty years ago a landowner out in his Delta estate found that the local foreman, the *ghafeer*, who had been commissioned to organize a duck shoot, had accidentally dropped the picnic hamper in an irrigation canal. Whereupon the following conversation took place. "You are a fool." "Yes, I am a fool, O Pasha." "You are a horse." "Yes, I am a horse, O Pasha." "You are a donkey." "Yes, I am a donkey, O Pasha." "So I curse you." "I am accursed, O Pasha." Then the two looked at each other in silence, until the *ghafeer* said, "I am a fool, O Pasha, and a horse, and a donkey, O Pasha. And I am accursed. But I have some eggs and bread in my house and I invite you." Whereupon the Pasha went to the *ghafeer's* house and stood with him in the little enclosure where a banana tree grew. They both ate, standing up and laughing.

In this curiously authoritarian society there is nevertheless a recognition that men are equal in the sight of God, and the acerbities of life are tempered with a recognition of common humanity. There is also a powerful sense of the ridiculous at work. The Pasha knew his insults were unreal and the maligned *ghafeer* was, in an odd sort of way, honoring the Pasha by simulating a fear and distress which, to be truthful, he did not feel. The powerful and the weak play games. This is not to deny an underlying ferocity. In a slightly different mood the Pasha might have struck the *ghafeer* over the head with the butt of his shotgun. But on this occasion he did not. Everything became a joke. When men are helpless, as they probably were under the Turks, a joke is the only alternative to despair.

Before the revolution of 1952 about one third of the cultivable land was owned by two thousand people. The rest was owned by small-holders with less than five acres each. It was part of the revolutionary aim to redistribute the land more widely. This was achieved but it does not necessarily mean that the older system dominated by big landowners was less efficient. One of the great problems of land tenure in Egypt results from the fact that Islamic law provided that at the death of the owner the land should be divided equally among the heirs; so that if a smallholder had six *feddans* (a *feddan* is slightly more than an acre) and three sons, each of them would inherit two *feddans*. The land was thus always being divided up into units that were not really economic. The big landowners were at least able to ensure that their land was farmed with a view to greatest productivity, no matter how offensive it might be to socialists that they were probably absentee landlords who lived in some splendor elsewhere, in Cairo or even in Europe. The splintering effect of the Islamic law was reduced by the need for some unified system that irrigation required. This is the thread that runs through Egyptian history—the need for cooperation that the distribution of the waters of the Nile imposes.

121

Now that the large landowners are no more, great efforts are being made to regroup farm fragments in a way that will make best use of the land. If, in the 1950's, you climbed to the top of a minaret outside Zagazig in the month of May you would see the Delta countryside like a patchwork quilt, with a strip of maize here, cotton there, with perhaps half a dozen children bending over the plants and removing the cotton-leaf worm by hand; and scattered patches where potatoes were being dug and onions harvested for export to Europe. And fruit orchards here and there. What is being attempted is the bringing together of the cotton fields, the maize patches, the rice fields, the vegetable gardens, and the orchards so that each can be farmed rationally, perhaps cooperatively. For one thing it will make it possible to use tractors and operate the irrigation canals more effectively. The traditional ways are not so easily changed, however, and an individual fellah may need a lot of persuading that it is to his advantage to sell his land to a cooperative and grow one crop instead of the three or four that he grew previously.

The peasant is eternally making and remaking small earth barriers (called *sadd*) to control the flow of water. The wheat field has to be watered four times during the six months from November to May, from its planting, that is, to harvest. Cotton is planted in February and watered at least eight times before it is picked in September and October, then to stand in great bales for the export market. Potatoes need even more water and so, naturally, does rice. The detail of this ritual came into existence when Nile waters were controlled to make irrigation possible throughout the year. Before that the Nile overflowed and grain was scattered broadcast on the mud. When the water receded the seeds were trodden in by animals turned out for that purpose or by pieces of wood dragged over the ground—as it is still done in parts of the Thebaid even today.

It was realized for a long time that the Nile water could be more widely distributed if the river was dammed, so raising the level of the water and conserving it. Mohammed Ali, the Albanian ruler, built a not very successful barrage, or dam, for this purpose north of Cairo and this was followed by a more successful one that brought considerable extra areas of land into cultivation. But a dam is a different and more dramatic concept. The original Aswan Dam was built in 1903 where some very hard rock cuts across the valley. This provided the base for the dam, which created a lake kept artificially low so as to preserve the ancient temples of Philae (which, even so, were largely submerged) and provoked a British journalist in 1899 to say that this is "a cruel, wicked, senseless sacrifice. . . . The state must struggle and the people must starve in order that professors may exult and tourists find some place on which to scratch their names." The journalist was Winston Churchill. The new High Dam that has been built is just south of this 1903 dam and will, by 1980, create a lake longer than England. Water flowed freely through the old Aswan Dam until October, by which time the silt had entirely gone through, to carry on down through Egypt the fertilizing process of a million years. The new High Dam will arrest the load of silt and this, presumably, will call for the use of more artificial manure. The advantage is that water can be released throughout the year in a way that will increase the area of land under cultivation. The hydroelectric power generated cannot fail to make Aswan a considerable industrial center.

Egypt, for the peasant, remains Nile mud. His house is Nile mud brick, formed in molds with an inmixing of straw and dried in the sun. His food is cooked in a Nile mud oven, and even his extravagant dovecotes,

The Egyptian peasant has from time immemorial worked on small parcels of land. There is now a move to bring the holdings together to allow for greater specialization of crops.

Upper Left. Farming implements and techniques have changed little over the centuries. In Pharaonic times the peasant following the plow drawn by two oxen would have used a plow made entirely of wood; nowadays it is usually, but not always, shod with steel.

Lower Left. The buffalo at the waterwheel is blindfolded and the wheel is metal, whereas up to fifty years ago it would have been of wood.

Left. The chief fodder crop for cattle and horses is berseem, *a kind of clover, which is grown in great rectangles of irrigated land, mainly in Upper Egypt, as here, near Assiut.*

Above. Some farm activities are a family affair—threshing spice crops, for example—in this instance with poles instead of flails.

Left. Sugar cane between Dendera and Abydos in Upper Egypt, where most of the sugar comes from. It had been introduced from the East by the first century A.D. Sugar is one of the two crops—cotton is the other—encouraged by Mohammed Ali at the beginning of the nineteenth century. The ancient Egyptians of Pharaonic times did not cultivate it.

Overleaf. Harvesting wheat is often done by hand—much the way it is shown in the ancient tomb paintings.

which look like white iced cakes, all pinnacles and ornately decorated, are Nile mud under the whitewash. The spectacle that has now gone is the sight of Egypt under water in August and September, with the villages, the mosques and their minarets and saints' tombs all on slight eminences sufficient to make them islands in the flood just as though—as Herodotus said—they were islands in the Aegean. Water nowadays is used less prodigally. It is (quite properly) controlled and allocated as the essential and scarce national resource it is. The modern peasant lives at a time when the blindfolded water buffalo who works his *sakiyeh* is insured by the state against illness and has a metal tab on its ear giving its state-registered number. If this sounds like too much bureaucracy, it has to be said that the nature of Egypt is such that from time immemorial cooperation and collaboration have been necessary to make civilized life possible. Nothing like the initiatives of the American frontier were ever remotely possible, if people in large numbers were to survive. From the earliest times the control and allocation of water have required the keeping of records, so that what worked one year can be expected to work the next. With a population of 80 million expected by the end of the century there is not a great deal of room for maneuver.

Creating Lake Nasser in Nubia meant that the two temples of Abu Simbel and the huge statues of Ramses II, his chief wife Nefertari, and other members of his family would be submerged. It was decided that they should be sliced out, like so much cheese, and moved to a point some sixty meters higher. This expensive and delicate operation was internationally financed. Ramses II would undoubtedly have thought it was the least he deserved. Such was his sense of the divine importance of his place in the cosmos that he himself is represented in four colossal statues; the rest of his family come up only to his knees, a symbolism with which they (if consulted, which was unlikely) would certainly have agreed. This great shrine was intended for the sun god. At sunrise light struck into the innermost sanctuary in a way that so played upon the statues that they seemed alive. These figures have long looked out over the valley and they are now, thanks to Egypt, UNESCO, and a West German engineering team, looking out over the waters of Lake Nasser which will play a great part in the future development of the country Ramses II ruled over more than 3,000 years ago.

Something like 40 percent of the Egyptian population now live in towns. People everywhere want to live in towns and cities because of the facilities city life provides, and the cities themselves (increasingly concerned with services of various kinds) require extra hands. Nevertheless, we must not forget that the heart of Egypt is agricultural. All depends on the man with his hoe turning the little ridge of earth so that the irrigating water flows this way one month and that way another. On an act as simple as this a complex civilization has depended.

There is no real evidence that the climate has changed significantly over the past 5,000 years, though the fact that grain was grown in parts of the Western Desert and in Cyrenaica where now is only desert may mean there was slightly more rain in Roman times. The tomb paintings and papyri record a greater wealth of plant and animal life than at present; the papyrus plant is now to be found only in the far south, in the Sudan, but the lotus, blue and white, still grows in the Delta and is prized as much as it was in Pharaonic times, when flowers played an important part in entertainment and ceremonials. The hippopotamus and crocodile have departed, but this is not for climatic reasons. There were more trees, but not enough, or of the right kind, to avoid the necessity for importing timber—cedar, juniper, and other conifers from Lebanon. The heat of July and August is mitigated in the Delta by "the sweet breath of the north wind," as the ancients called it, and in the south of the country by the dryness of the air. But it does get hot. Temperatures of well over 100° F. are registered at Aswan in the summer. It is less in the north of the country but even so the peasant labors for many months of the year in temperatures that only necessity and custom make tolerable. In the early summer there are sometimes hot and dusty winds from the southwest called the *khamseen* (from the Arabic for "fifty," this being the number of days when it is liable to blow) which are very disagreeable indeed. The wind is sometimes violent, the air is so thick with the dust the sun is obscured, and all one is aware of is an amber glow from the sky; the temperature rockets up and little flies appear from nowhere to cling to one's face. Murderers have been known to plead, in mitigation of their crime, that it was committed during the *khamseen*. But except for the heat of high summer the climate of Egypt is mostly glorious and, in the winter, as enjoyable as any in the world; a never-failing sun, blue sky, and a gentle breeze.

Egypt is the Mediterranean as well as Africa. It grows grapes in the north and from the earliest times made wine. In the south the Egyptians grew dates, melons, wheat, and barley. Barley was used for bread and the brewing of beer. Whether one got drunk on wine or on beer, the general view was that this was a good thing. A drunken man is out of ordinary life and in communion with the gods. Modern Egypt is, of course, a predominantly Moslem country. To the orthodox Moslem alcohol is forbidden. But the cultural richness of Egypt's past is not to be channeled through any narrow orthodoxy, and of all Moslems the Egyptians are the most easygoing. The ancient Egyptian regarded the desert Arab as a barbarian and this attitude has lasted through the centuries. Until as recently as twenty years ago the educated Egyptian, if asked to declare his identity, would talk in terms of Egypt, of Africa, and of the Mediterranean. Religion and language tug toward Mecca but one has the feeling that the innate genius of the country will in the future see it playing a more individual role.

It was fashionable at one time for Europeans to compare the town Egyptian unfavorably with the Bedouin of the desert. Wilfrid Scawen Blunt was one of those Victorian Englishmen who identified themselves with nationalist movements in various parts of the world. In Egypt he was a strong defender of Arabi Pasha, but he carried his anti-imperialist views so far as to dress as a desert Arab in Cairo. As the desert Arabs, or Bedouins, were regarded as a rough lot by cultured Egyptian society, Blunt's behavior was thought eccentric. The Egyptian Bedouins nowadays are not numerous. It has been calculated that there are no more than about 50,000 of them all told. Since Blunt's

In an open-air market in Cairo women are buying tomatoes.

time there has been a change in the attitude of the educated Egyptian toward these nomadic tribesmen. They are now sometimes seen, romantically, as enjoying a free and natural life not possible in the Nile Valley. In the Egyptian cinema and novels a Bedouin love interest provides color and magic the city dweller does not see around him; yet he believes it to be genuinely Egyptian and related to his own aspirations in the same way that cowboy movies are regarded by the American.

The nomadic, pastoral way of life was thought to be a natural development from hunting and fruit-gathering societies, but it is more likely that it sprang from an agricultural way of life. Population pressure caused little groups to hive off from settled communities based on cultivation, rather as the patriarch Abraham led his people out of Ur in Lower Mesopotamia. He is the archetypal Bedouin leader, with his tents, his flocks, and his sublime self-confidence. The Bedouins of Egypt lead a life not so very dissimilar to his. They move along the edge of cultivation, either of the Nile Valley or of the great oases, breeding and selling camels, constantly moving on with their goats and sheep, perhaps even planting wheat where conditions permit and returning months later to gather the undoubtedly wretched harvest. The nomad drinks strong black coffee, flavored perhaps with cardamom, on the side of his tent away from the wind and therefore left open. Here is his carpet and coffee hearth, where the head of the family is ready to prepare the coffee himself, the one domestic chore he deigns to take on. The women have often been unveiled and there are times when they dress splendidly with bracelets, ankle rings with bells, and even, if they are well off, with a display of coins across the bust. In this manner they are sometimes to be seen, with their menfolk, coming in from the desert through the palm groves with young camels for sale.

The settled population of the oases is quite different. It has been an admixture of Berber stock, which is different from the Arab or the Egyptian. The Berbers are spread throughout North Africa. They have their own language and writing and are sometimes described as having red hair and blue eyes by writers anxious to establish some northern origin for this people; fair hair and blue eyes are rare. What is certainly true is that they have been in the region of North Africa from time immemorial and were known to the ancient Egyptians, who had a number of names for them, such as Libu and Kahaka. But the visitor to the oases nowadays is not likely to be greatly struck by an extreme contrast of physical types with those he has left behind him in the Nile Valley. There has been so much coming and going over the years. Even so, the Berber language is spoken (Arabic as well) by a population that depends mainly on various kinds of agriculture for its living—notably of dates. Of dates there are many varieties. The dates of Siwa are reputed to be better than any other, though the dark dates from the northwest of the Delta, which are very succulent and can be eaten fresh, are hard to surpass.

The visitor to Cairo or the holiday maker in Upper Egypt is likely to be confused as between Berbers and the men who come downstream from Nubia to be servants, doorkeepers, or cooks and who are sometimes referred to as Barabra. They are in fact Nubians and their language has nothing to do with Berber or Arabic. They are a handsome, honest, and honorable people who look very smart in their spotlessly clean white gowns and headcloths as they steer a felucca on the Upper Nile or bring in one's coffee at the tourist hotel. After they have made enough money in Egypt they go back to their homes once south of Aswan—but now in Upper Egypt displaced by

Lake Nasser—there to settle. In this they are rather like Syrian and Lebanese Arabs who at one time used to make their fortunes in North America, eventually to return to their native mountains and ride about on powerful donkeys splendidly arrayed in embroidered waistcoats and baggy black trousers.

The great question is to what extent the basic Egyptian characteristics have been modified by invasion and dominance by aliens. Clearly the sense that all was fundamentally right with the universe, *maat*, must have been changed by evidence that one's rulers acted in an arbitrary and tyrannical way—as, no doubt, the Persians in the sixth century B.C. did. The Persians were still in control when Herodotus arrived in about 455 B.C. from Greece. The Greeks, and even more the Romans and their Byzantine successors, must have created the impression that, so far as the ordinary Egyptian was concerned, the fundamental ordering of the universe had been interrupted. It is no wonder that the Egyptians were particularly receptive to Christianity. The old Egyptian religions saw temporal and spiritual power as two aspects of the same fundamental truth. When temporal power became a dream so far as Egyptians were concerned, a spiritual teaching which made use of many of the traditional Egyptian doctrines was very nearly irresistible. Implicit in the native religions was the concept of a transcendent god, Amon-Re. Isis, the mother god, who was represented with the infant Horus on her lap, was easily subsumed in the Virgin Mary. The concept of Logos, the Word "by whom all things are made," was related to the god Ptah as the god of language through whom all awareness came into existence.

Whatever continuity one might detect from the religious beliefs and practices of the ancient Egyptians to Christianity and the present dominant faith of the country, Islam, there is one belief that petered out when Egypt was a province of Byzantium—a religious emphasis on animals. Whole cemeteries of mummified cats have been discovered. The crocodile was venerated and on death embalmed and placed in sacred coffers. Falcons and bulls also came in for this treatment, and many of the animal cults seem to have been a way of expressing awareness of fundamental forces working through the agency of animals—the bull Apis was a manifestation of Osiris, the crocodile god Sobek was associated with the rising of the Nile, Thoth the god of learning was seen as an ibis. The scale of this practice amazed the rest of the ancient world and many explanations for it have been put forward.

Other races have animals as totems; certain Hindu sects have such a veneration for life that even the swatting of a fly is forbidden, and the sacred cows of India survive to this day. But the Egyptian attitude toward animals was neither totemic nor entirely irrational—unless just liking animals is thought to be irrational, for that must have been a strong element in the cult. One has only to see the loving care with which the wildlife of the country is naturalistically and beautifully represented in paintings. In the Cairo Museum there is a tomb painting from the IVth Dynasty showing, on a gray background, superbly painted and brilliantly colored geese. Everywhere, in the tombs and in papyrus drawings, ducks are seen rising from the marshes, ibis stalk in the fields, fish swim, pelicans, cranes, hares, monkeys, cats abound—all shown for what they are without any religious significance. Not only did the Egyptians like animals, they were amused by them. In Turin there are papyrus drawings showing animals with musical instruments, a donkey playing a harp, a lion a lyre, a baboon with a double flute, and a crocodile beating time with a long-necked stringed instrument over one arm; meanwhile a cat is attacked by a

1.

2.

3.

4.

5.

6.

8.

9.

The women of Egypt have large, strikingly beautiful eyes, nearly always brown, but very occasionally blue, indicating Berber blood: 1. the young child learning to weave at a tapestry school in Haranaya; 2. the artist's model posing for painter Hassan Soliman in Cairo; 3. the television actress Nagawe Abrahim on her "Birds of Paradise" show; 4. the girl near the tomb of Nakht; 7. and the Cairo businesswoman Mona Korashy all have these large and luminous eyes. 10. So has the village woman who walks through the palm groves where Memphis once stood.

10.

Water carrying, craft work, construction, and dancing have always been widespread activities in Egypt: 5. a woman carries her unglazed pot near Kena, a famous pottery-making center, in Upper Egypt; 6. another weaves an intricate design at the tapestry school in Haranaya; 9. another balances a load of mud for making bricks at Rosetta; 8. and the girls perform a folk dance at the Balloon Theatre in Cairo.

Egyptian men are generally thin and are normally clean-shaven though most have a mustache. The Coptic monk with the ancient missal is at St. Anthony's Monastery in the Eastern Desert; such monks have always been venerated. The architect Hassan Fathi looks as Imhotep himself might have looked, and there are certainly musicians in the tomb reliefs like those at the Nile Hilton nightclub.

duck and a blackbird climbs a ladder to steal fruit from a tree, only to find a miniature hippopotamus waiting for it.

The cult of animals went beyond mere liking. Although he does not say so (indeed, he goes out of his way to avoid explaining why the Egyptians accounted all animals sacred) Herodotus does write about reincarnation. The Egyptian priests told him that the immortality of the soul was a doctrine first taught in Egypt in ancient times; when the body died the soul entered into another creature then coming to birth—a duck or a cat, maybe—and so on through a three-thousand-year cycle before the soul re-entered the human body once more. This was a doctrine that Pythagoras, the Greek philosopher, who almost certainly visited Egypt about 70 years before Herodotus, adopted into his theory of metempsychosis. But whatever the priests told Herodotus there is no real evidence that the Egyptians expected to be reincarnated into animals and we cannot argue that such a belief was related to the importance given to birds and beasts.

The fact is that from the most ancient times there were animal cults in Egypt which sprang from real or imagined qualities in the animal venerated—for example, the Apis bulls of Sakkara and the Mnevis bulls of Heliopolis. In the course of time animals associated with certain deities were mummified and placed in cemeteries or catacombs within a temple precinct. At Bubastis, city of the cat goddess Bastet, one finds cat mummies. At Hermopolis, home of Thoth, whose animals were the ibis and the baboon, one finds ibis catacombs and a few mummified baboons—few because they were more expensive to buy. What had started out, in the earliest pre-dynastic times, as a kind of totemism, eventually became a cult in which mummified animals were offered to the temples as votives, not entirely dissimilar from the way modern Catholics buy and light candles.

More fundamental reasons for the Egyptian veneration of animals have been put forward, notably by Henri Frankfort. He said that they played an important role in Egyptian religion because they were alive as humans were alive, but differently; in an animal the human being recognized an *otherness*. This recognition exists in all specifically religious feeling. Moreover, animals do not change. Generation after generation they are the same. The first wearer of the double crown of Egypt in 3000 B.C., would see the "same" duck that Ramses II saw more than a millennium and a half afterwards. Animals, in their apparent changelessness, were an expression of the static world order which was a basic assumption of priest and peasant.

One wonders. The theory turns on an assumption that priests and peasants were conscious of living in a static society which reflected a fundamental truth about the created universe. The probability is that no Egyptian could have formulated such a view. To do that would require a knowledge of some evolutionary theory of history for comparison.

Most of the beards one sees in the tomb paintings are the artificial ones worn by the Pharaoh as a sign of his divinity and power. Although the men are shown with splendid heads of hair these were usually wigs; and they were clean-shaven unlike other ancient peoples —the Assyrians, the Babylonians, and the Persians. In the Tigris-Euphrates Valley and on the Iranian plateau the men had splendid, full, crinkled black beards. Not for the Pharaoh the natural hirsutic virtuosity of the Chaldeans or even the Hebrews. His artificial beard was as much part of the royal insignia as the double crown, the uraeus worn centrally above the forehead, the flail, and the scepter. Even today a full-bearded Egyptian is a rarity; but mustaches are so common it is evident that beards could be worn.

139

At Edfu, in Upper Egypt, is the best-preserved Egyptian temple. But across the road, outside a somewhat dilapidated house, domestic life of the present day goes on. A young woman feeds her baby while other members of her family keep her company. What does she care of Horus (whose temple she could see if she lifted her eyes) or the ancient splendor of Egypt?

The skin of an Egyptian can be very light or very dark indeed and it is customary to relate the coloring to the degree of latitude— fairest in the north, browner in the south—but the generalization is only broadly true today. There has been so much movement of population. Certainly the fellaheen who work in the fields are darker than the storekeeper or teacher but that is because they are out in the sun all day; and they are darker, too, than their more stay-at-home wives. In the tomb paintings men were often shown red and women white or yellow, for the same reason. Their eyes—almost invariably brown— can be full and beautiful in women, particularly in young women; the men have a more hooded expression, and the fellaheen in particular have a habit of keeping their eyes half closed and lowering their eyebrows in a way that seems to be an expression of displeasure but is really no more than what one has to do in bright sunlight without tinted glasses. Egyptians suffer from many diseases of the eye— trachoma, glaucoma, and others brought on by the lack of hygiene in many parts of the country, though enormous improvements have been made over the past few years. A not uncommon mark of the Egyptian is an eye defect.

There are not many fat Egyptians, though plumpness is an admired quality, within limits, in women, not necessarily by women themselves. The Egyptian man, as he goes about his work, gives the impression of strength and scrawniness. If long-distance running ever became a national sport in Egypt, which is unlikely, the Egyptians might well become very good at it, as they are already at swimming and squash. Maybe they will become good at soccer, too, which is already developing into a national cult. Egyptians present their bodies well. Women walk erectly like queens because, it is said, they are accustomed to carrying burdens on their heads. And this is true: water jars, bales of fodder, provisions from the market are all balanced on the head and transported with elegance. But men walk well, too, in their loose turbans and long gowns, called galabiehs, which can be of simple cotton for the poorest or brocaded silk for the rich. In towns Western dress is more often worn, until recently very often with the red felt rimless hat, the tarboosh, which was a Turkish innovation— a more inappropriate headgear for a hot climate it would be hard to imagine. Civil servants—and there are many of them in Egypt—wore the tarboosh as a sign of their status. It was the mark of the effendi— the intellectual, businessman, entrepreneur, journalist, professional man—and indeed there was a whole language of the tarboosh which used to be exploited in the Egyptian comic theater. Everything depended on how the tassel was worn. If it was worn, in a farouche sort of way, over the front of the tarboosh, it meant that the wearer was angry, if at the left side one thing, if at the right another. A man of conventional habits wore his tassel at the back. But all this has gone, even during the past twenty years or so. The tarboosh was actually banned in Turkey, but in Egypt it has largely fallen out of use because it was too much identified with a certain class and outlook.

In the twentieth century Egyptians have made distinguished contributions in many fields of knowledge, particularly medicine, education, architecture, and engineering. The lives and outlook of leading professional people in Egypt are more Western or European than in any other Arab state, but they seem to be concentrated in Cairo, which is still seen as the inevitable center of all political and intellectual life.

Apart from Cairo, the great cities of Egypt, Alexandria and Port Said, were more cosmopolitan before the last war than they are today. There was a great inflow of foreigners during the nineteenth century, particularly from Greece, Italy, France, Spain, and, to a lesser extent,

Britain. These foreigners enjoyed privileged legal status. They were not subject to the ordinary Moslem law of Egypt but enjoyed what were known as Capitulations, the right to be tried for offenses in their own consular courts. These legal privileges were ended long ago but substantial foreign colonies remained. The year of the Franco-British invasion of the Suez Canal Zone, 1956, was the great watershed. After that many holders of foreign passports left the country. As a consequence, the feel of these cities is much more Arab than it was a generation ago. There have been Jews in Egypt for thousands of years and there are still synagogues in Cairo.

Foreigners who lived in Egypt in the Twenties and Thirties must, if they still survive, be rather elderly now. "You have no idea," they are capable of saying, "how delightful life was then." Much of the delight came from the privileged position they occupied. Living was cheap, servants were plentiful, and officialdom was helpful even to the point of being deferential. In Cairo, Alexandria, and Port Said there were excellent clubs. The Mohammed Ali Club in Cairo was much frequented by rich Egyptians who liked to gamble. The Turf Club was a stronghold of the British, and burned down as such. The Anglo-Egyptian Union shared a large and beautiful garden with the Egyptian Army Officers' Club, premises where much of the talk leading up to the Revolution took place. But most important of all was the Gezireh Sporting Club where all manner of games—polo, golf, squash, tennis—could and still can be played. The Egyptians love horse-racing. There are courses in Cairo itself, in Gezireh next to the Sporting Club, and at Heliopolis and Alexandria.
Although the Sporting Club still flourishes, the old club life has disappeared. Egypt is no longer a land of privileges for the few. The economic difficulties of the country are real and they become almost palpable in the streets by reason of the very press of people. Cairo is a teeming city. The streetcars and buses are not only full, they are festooned with people who would rather travel on the roof or by hanging on to the side than not travel at all. They are extraordinarily good humored and patient with one another as, through the many centuries, they have always been.

The Christian Wave: Coptic Monks

Christianity seems to have been congenial in the Delta and Nile Valley and it gave a powerful stimulus to Egyptian nationalism. It restated old Egyptian insights and represented them with the same symbolism. Isis, the mother goddess, held the infant Horus in her arms and it became natural to represent the Virgin Mary and the infant Jesus in this iconography of Isis and Horus. To a devout Egyptian of the early centuries A.D., Christian doctrine exposed the essential truth about existence; folk memory was transformed into a living experience by the good news that God was love, and suffered, as ordinary men and women did under Roman imperialism—for Egypt became a plundered province, valued mainly for its wealth and grain—and out of this religious experience came nationalism. The Egyptians were exploited and oppressed by the Romans and their Byzantine successors. It was natural, in the Egyptian mind, for this economic and political drive to translate itself into arguments about fundamental belief and church structures. The true believer who could find no satisfaction in being an ordinary member of society turned his back on it. Some devout Christians went into the desert and lived a life of austere contemplation.

Christian monasticism arose in Egypt. There were Essene monastic institutions in Palestine before Jesus was born, and in India the Buddhist hermit and monk had existed for generations; at the heart of Buddhism was a wrestling with illusion—a wrestling that led to the rejection of too obvious a happiness in favor of austerities which could be counted more real. Egyptian Christian monasticism may have owed something to the East but it is more likely to have been indigenous. The evolution of the Egyptian personality from the time when *maat* was taken to be the ground of one's being to the period when key individuals, like St. Anthony, could save their souls only by rejecting the world is one of the most arresting times in cultural history and must have been an expression of deep suffering by the Egyptian people.

The urge to leave the village or town and live apart in ascetic self-discipline is not something one finds record of in earlier periods of Egyptian history. The development can only have come about because of the impact made by the Christian message on Egyptians who felt that the world they lived in was corrupt, was one whose ends they could feel no confidence in shaping and which, in any case, or so they believed, was shortly to come to an end. The Christian doctrines of death and judgment caused many ostentatiously to reject Caesar in favor of God. St. Anthony was a Copt who, at the age of twenty, heard in church the words of the Gospel of St. Matthew—"Sell that thou hast . . ."—did precisely that, gave the proceeds to the poor, and went to the desert to fast, fight demons, and subject himself to all the mortifications of the flesh. Unlike his ancestors who believed there was a moral order in the universe one could aspire to share by observing a need for justice and fairness in one's life, St. Anthony saw life as a struggle to achieve, through the mortification of the flesh, enough grace to be saved at the last.

With all the enthusiasm of the newly initiated the young Copts made for the desert in such numbers that a report at the end of the fourth century said, erroneously no doubt, that half the male population of Egypt were monks, anchorites, or hermits. The personality of Anthony drew enthusiasts after him. His cave is still shown near the monastery named after him in the Eastern desert south of Suez. Another great monastic center was the Thebaid in Upper Egypt, where Pachomius was the first to organize monks under strict discipline with manual labor, craft work, and education. Egyptian nationalism came to the surface in the person of St. Shenoute, who

145

The unglazed pots of Ballas in Upper Egypt are famous. Known as Kena pottery, they are made from local clay. Some of these pots, or balalis, *are big enough for a man to get into (as in "Ali Baba and the Forty Thieves") but most are medium-sized water pots, or* kullehs, *which are porous, so allowing water to sweat through and evaporate — a natural cooling process.*

Right. The turkey is a North American bird that has done well in Egypt and become so mild-mannered that even a boy can handle it, as here in the Faiyum.

Above. In this Delta interior the door is more substantial than the mud brick of the walls. The diet includes little meat. Flat loaves of bread, or merahah, *are the basis for most meals.*

Overleaf. In the Delta it may rain in winter, and villages made of mud brick, like this one near Rosetta, must be constantly repaired. Maize straw is used for roofing.

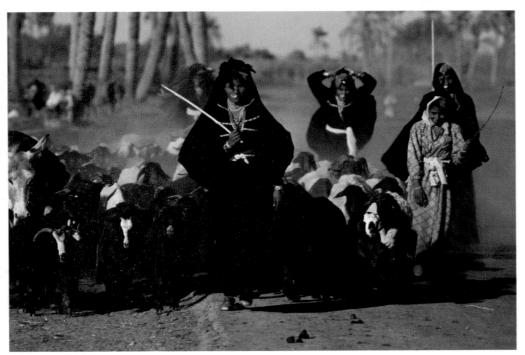

*Upper Left. Until the mid-
nineteenth century a deliberate
policy of tree planting was not
established. These* lebbakh *trees
provide shade in the Delta.
Lower Left. In the province of
Faiyum, Bedouin women can be
seen wearing brass nose rings
and leading goats and sheep.
Above. The simple, somber
garment of the Egyptian country-
woman is called a* helaliyeh. *It
is voluminous and, considering
the climate, is wrapped around
the body more for modesty
than for comfort.*

Left. Behind the fellah on his mule is the Chephren Pyramid at Giza, looking a little like the fan of light that can break through a cloud when the sun's rays are at a certain angle. This may be a reason why the form had special significance to the Egyptians. Overleaf. The sheep, cattle, and camel market at Luxor brings in farmers from the surrounding villages, not only to trade but also to exchange news.

but the universal food is brown beans, called *fool,* which are slowly cooked all night in an earthenware pot and served with oil. Out of necessity the Egyptian diet is largely vegetarian and this may have something to do with the lack of superfluous flesh on their bodies.

Water is treated with great respect. It all comes from the Nile so there is not the possibility of developing a discriminating palate as in, say, Istanbul where connoisseurs at one time prided themselves on saying which well their drink had been brought from. But in Egypt a cool drink is always welcome, and since the clay pots in which it is stored are always being broken, there is a thriving industry in *kullehs,* as the pots are called. There is no shortage of the right kind of clay and these water containers are never glazed. Some pots have a narrow neck and a kind of brass nozzle that allows the water to be poured with precision. The art is to lift one of these *doraks* onto your shoulder and tilt the pot in such a way that a jet of water falls cleanly into your mouth, without the nozzle touching the lips. Visitors unaccustomed to the art get wet.

Egyptians have a high mechanical aptitude and not only successfully operate the various automobile assembly plants that are to be found in the country but also maintain a high standard of craft work in glassware, leather goods, metalwork, and faience. The once luxurious Shepheard's Hotel was built with local skills in the 1950's in all its detail, from the execution of the major architectural design down to the making of individual locks, window fittings, lampshades, tables, chairs, beds, furnishings, and linen. In part this indigenous labor was brought about by restrictions on imports but in the main it was due to the enterprise of the Arab architect, Elie Chagoury, who was determined to show what Egyptian craftsmen were capable of. Cloth is woven and tapestry made using the same techniques as in Pharaonic Egypt, so there was no difficulty in this area. The complicated latticework of the screens to be seen in some of the reception rooms is an old Egyptian craft; this is how the screens in Coptic churches and *mushrabiya* windows were made. Chagoury's particular triumph was to design colored-glass windows and have them, too, executed in a local factory.

Mosques and Fatimid Masters

Left. The earliest mosques had no minaret. The mosque of Ibn-Tulun was completed in 879 A.D. and has a minaret unique in Egypt. Ibn-Tulun came from Samarra, north of Baghdad, where the great Friday mosque has a spiral stair around the outside of the minaret. The unusual means of ascent was probably inspired by this minaret at Samarra; and the malwiya *at Samarra was, in turn, inspired by the ancient Babylonian ziggurats, or temple towers.*

Overleaf. The austere beauty of Ibn-Tulun's mosque was intended to free the mind for the calm contemplation of God. The great sahn, *or courtyard, is surrounded by arcades.*

There is no way of proving that Islam, when it came to Egypt as a result of the conquest by an Arab general, Amr ibn-al-As, just before the middle of the seventh century A.D., owed anything in its practice to Coptic Christianity, but it does seem reasonable to suppose that the example of the desert monks and anchorites made an impression on the newcomers. It is wrong to suppose that they were fierce prose-lytizers who offered non-believers the alternative of the Faith or the sword. That ferocity came later and was truer of the Turks than of the Arabs, who seem to have been respectful to other peoples of the Book, as they considered both Jews and Christians to be. The control of Egypt was initially tolerant. There were movements, within Islam, to emphasize the spiritual and mystic insights of the Prophet. Orders were established, not entirely dissimilar to Christian orders. It was part of the Prophet's teaching that a great gap separated man from God, but certain of the orders of dervishes, as they came to be called, emphasized a more personal relationship with the deity and even, through revelation and ecstasy, a union of the soul with God. One of the earliest and greatest of Moslem mystics was an Egyptian, Dun 'l-Nan al-Misti. He was a member of one of the Sufi brotherhoods that still exist in Egypt. He died in the ninth century and his tomb can still be seen in Cairo. Was he a converted Copt? He was reputed to be able to read hieroglyphs and was the first in Islam to teach the doctrine of *ma'rifa*, which would not have seemed alien to his Christian contemporaries and meant acquiring knowledge of spiritual matters through illumination and ecstasy. The language of love and wine was used to talk of the holy mysteries, as in the Christian eucharist.

Many people have written about the survival into Moslem times and the modern world of certain practices which owe their origin to the time of the Pharaohs. The Christian Church has an impressive record of taking over pagan festivals for its own good purposes; the birth of Christ is celebrated on December 25, in the Western Church, not because Jesus was actually born at this time (it is unlikely) but be-because this was a Mithraic feast in the Roman world, the birthday of the unconquered sun. There are no precise equivalents to this in Islam, but the Egyptian spring holiday of Sham el-Nesim (it means "the smelling of the Zephyr"), when everyone goes out into the fields and open places to eat fish and other delicacies, has been seen as a survival of a Pharaonic practice of celebrating the rebirth of the Phoenix. There are religious feasts in honor of some Moslem or Christian saint which still go on—though not so much as even fifty years ago—which do not seem everything the celebrators believe them to be, the one at Luxor, for example, where boats that look extraordinarily like Pharaonic boats are dragged on carts in proces-sion. Could this be some shadowy relic of the ancient Egyptian water festival of Opet, when the god Amon sailed upstream to his shrine in the Luxor temple? The so-called "bride of the Nile," a doll thrown into the rising waters of the Nile in Cairo at the critical moment, is certainly ancient. How much does this matter?

It matters less than the fact that everyone speaks Arabic. There were special reasons for the success of the language. The Koran is in Arabic, religious celebrations in any language other than Arabic would have been thought heretical, and the verbal impulse that was associ-ated with the religious certainty proved irresistible. The occupation of Egypt by Islam was ideological as well as a matter of mere mili-tary power and administrative imperatives. Sura 7 of the Koran says: "Every nation has its appointed time and when their appointed time

169

comes they cannot keep it back an hour, nor can they bring it on."
So it was with the Arabs. Their particular genius is for words. The
Koran itself, apart from its religious significance, is a great work of
Arabic literature and its regular reading aloud proved irresistible to
the Egyptian ear. Because of this religious imperative or because the
power was in the hands of the Arabs, the Egyptian language began
a slow decline. In the early eighth century A.D. Arabic replaced
Coptic as the official language for public documents.

In Islam the truth is expressed only through the Word. As among the
Hebrews, representational art, whether of men or of God, was
heresy. The icon was blasphemy, the statue an impiety. The Holy
Scriptures alone were appropriate for the decoration of buildings.
The Arabic script, particularly in the highly stylized form known as
Kufic (from Kufa in Mesopotamia, where it was developed), lent
itself to this adornment of stone and it soon, like later Arab scripts,
blossomed into complex formal intricacies. Pattern and decoration
were not, however, an end in themselves. Their contemplation was
an aid to the religious experience.

The mosque is an expression of a religious discipline and of a temperament. Its basic function is to create an atmosphere of calm and concentration so that the faithful can, in their devotions, have some sense
of communion with the One God. The mosque of Ibn-Tulun in Cairo,
which is one of the oldest places of prayer in Moslem Egypt, has this
simplicity. It is a thousand years old and a building that, more than
most of the buildings one can think of, conduces to repose and
magnanimity. It is a glory of human endeavor. This particular
mosque has a minaret like no other in Egypt. The building was
inspired by the great mosque of Samarra, north of Baghdad, where
there is a remarkable minaret separate from the mosque itself and
a spiral path to the top ascending on the outside of the structure.
This was inspired in turn by the ziggurat temples of ancient Babylonia and Sumer. No matter how highly decorated and elaborately
furnished mosques were later to become, they remained functional
buildings; the minaret was ascended to call the faithful to prayer, the
building was oriented so that they knew the direction of Mecca, there
was a well for ablutions and a pulpit so that the speaker could command his audience. No part of the building was more sacred than
another. There was no architectural symbolism. There was no catering
to any priestly mystery. God was not so easily approached. All
one could do was construct an enclosure in which the mind was not
distracted and the devout could give themselves to prayer.

Cairo has the most remarkable concentration of Islamic religious buildings to be found anywhere. About a hundred years after Ahmad Ibn-
Tulun built his great mosque the country was conquered by the
Fatimids in 969 (so called because they claimed descent from the
Prophet's daughter Fatima) and it was they who founded the city of
Cairo. Their oldest surviving building is the mosque of Al Azhar,
which became the great medieval university of Islam with students
coming from all parts of the Moslem world. Under the Fatimids, Cairo
became a great cultural center. This was the time when Greek
philosophical and scientific literature was translated into Arabic and,
since Fatimid power stretched from Arabia through North Africa to
Sicily, was in some measure fed back into European thinking.

A potentate of the Middle Ages, who lives on in the imagination is the
Fatimid Caliph al-Hakim. He had a disordered mind and loved riding
about in the dark on his ass inspecting the behavior of his subjects
as Haroun al-Raschid had been reputed to do not so very long before
in Baghdad. The part of Cairo with which he is most associated
the Mokattam Hills, particularly the slopes to the south of
the Citadel where now there are modern blocks of apartments and

172

Left. The eastern side of Cairo is a "city of the dead," for there, under the Citadel and the Mokattam Hills, the medieval rulers of Egypt had their cemeteries and mausoleums. The tombs of the so-called Caliphs are in fact tombs of the Circassian Mamelukes. Many of these mausoleums have fallen into disrepair. There are more modest tombs, with small courtyards and rooms, where relatives of the dead come at certain times of the year. Overleaf. The domes of Cairo mosques lack the ornate, bejeweled quality of Persian and Iraqi mosques but they have a monumental dignity. The tomb mosque of Sultan Barkuk, completed about 1410, was the first with a stone dome. The finest tomb, that of Kait Bey, built in 1463, has tiger stripes, an exquisite minaret, a courtyard, and a four-porched madrasa. *The Pharaohs were buried on the west bank of the Nile; their Arab and Turkish successors were buried east of the river. The significance of the west as the land of the dead had disappeared with the old religions.*

a rough road that leads to the monastery of the Baktashe Dervishes. He used to ride here in very simple attire, sometimes quite alone. This was a foolhardy thing to do, for his wanton killings made him an object of considerable hatred and it is remarkable that his assassination was postponed as long as it was. He belonged not to the orthodox sect of Islam, the Sunni, but to the Shia sect, which has a tendency toward emphasizing the personal understanding of God. The Shia sect has produced more mystics than the orthodox line in Islam and an extreme form of this mysticism attached to al-Hakim. A new doctrine arose in which he was proclaimed God. Egypt is a land where the kings had been gods in the past, but to Moslems, whose orthodox faith placed a distance between God and men, it is particularly abhorrent to deify men: so when in 1020 a preacher in the mosque of 'Amr, the most ancient in Egypt, said, "In the name of al-Hakim, the Compassionate, the Merciful," there was outrage and riot. Hakim's mother was an Orthodox Christian whose influence on Hakim had been strong. The Christian doctrine of the Incarnation, which owed so much to the Egyptian past, would have been familiar to Hakim and in some distorted way understood to have special application to himself. It was almost as though in his solitary wanderings he saw himself as a martyr on the grand scale, one who could be sacrificed for the good of creation.

What happened to him in the end is mysterious. In February 1021 he rode out on his ass in the direction of the Mokattam Hills at nightfall and was never seen again. He joined that mysterious company of heroes who are expected to return, like King Arthur, at a time of special danger or significance; and to this day the Druses of Lebanon believe that he will come again in majesty and apocalyptic splendor.

It is impossible to walk in the dusty wastes of eastern Cairo, above the City of the Dead, particularly at nightfall, and not think of this strange, taciturn man, half expecting at the turn of some sandy flank of the hill to see him sitting well back on his donkey, with no jewel in his turban and no decoration on his plain gray robe, riding in silence, eyes looking straight ahead, intent on some suprahuman destiny. He was a patron of the arts and sciences. His Institute of Advanced Studies (to give it a modern name) no longer exists but it was a real building erected in 1005 with the idea of promoting learning. Al-Hakim was only an extreme form of that recurrent type of Egyptian ruler during the Middle Ages, and later, the man who built splendid mosques and institutes of learning but at the same time was racked by suspicion and killed as a psychopath. His mosque is one of those the guide never fails to point out to tourists near the Bab en-Nasr.

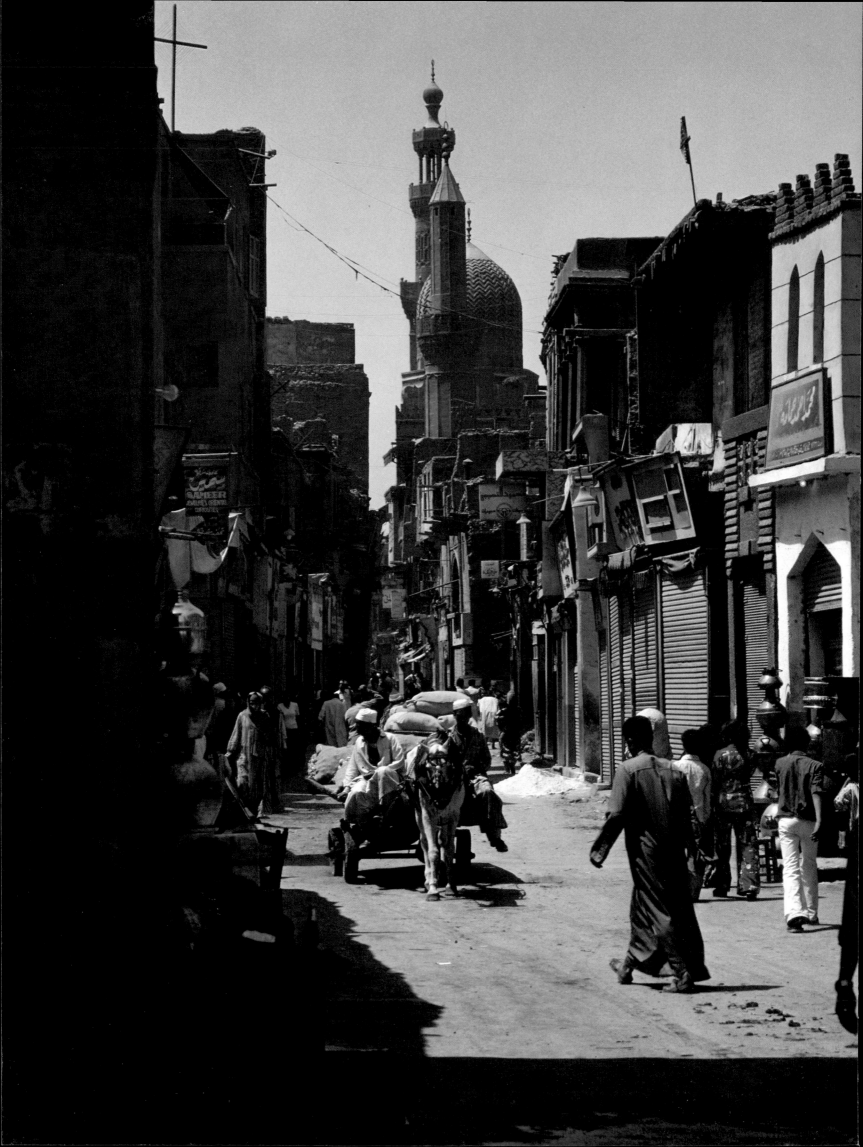

Mameluke Rulers and Moslem Rituals

What, one wonders, was the attitude of the ordinary Egyptian in the Middle Ages toward government? The most agreeable way to find out is to read the *Thousand and One Nights*, where, no matter what the provenance of the story, it is Egypt itself—particularly the Egypt of the Mamelukes—that provided the detail of daily life and, more important, the attitude toward power. No mistake about it, the belief was that power is arbitrary. The provincial farmer would hope to keep as free from entanglements as possible. In the cities, particularly Cairo, the merchants and traders would put up their shutters, or even close the gates that divided quarter from quarter, while the factions fought for power. It was alien power. If, in the late Middle Ages, an Egyptian were asked who had been the great men of Egypt, he would probably have replied Alexander the Greek, Saladin the Kurd, and Baybars the Mameluke—a slave, that is, from somewhere between the Caspian Sea and the Ural Mountains, in what is now the Soviet Union. They were all foreigners.

To be foreign is a fairly modern concept and the fact that their rulers came from countries to the north was probably of less importance to the Egyptians than their religion, which was Moslem—though their bad Arabic may have been a consideration. These sultans were great soldiers, and military prowess won acclaim even from the unmilitaristic peasants and merchants of Egypt. Saladin is well known to us because he was the great adversary in the Crusades and, rather confusingly, showed himself to be more magnanimous and civilized than the rough soldiery from Europe, who were mostly on the make rather than inspired by any religious feeling.

The Citadel overlooking Cairo from the east was built by Saladin as a means of controlling Egypt after the Fatimid Dynasty ended in 1171. To stand on its ramparts today and look west over the greatest city in Africa is to have a perspective on most of Egyptian history. In the middle distance is a flash from the Nile if the sun is at the right angle. Beyond that, remotely to the southwest, can be picked out, twenty miles away, if the haze permits, the Step Pyramid at Sakkara. The eye moves north to the Pyramids of Giza—stuck like cardboard models against a backcloth of desert—what the ancient Egyptians called Deshre, the Red Land, in contrast to the black of the cultivable land. To the right of the Pyramids again, beyond the dark green of palm trees, is the point where the desert road to Alexandria starts on its 120-mile journey, passing Wadi Natroun and the Coptic monasteries in their valley.

On this side of the Nile, to the south are the deserted wastes that mark the first Arab city in Egypt, al-Fustat, which predates Cairo itself by 300 years, and Old Cairo with its Coptic churches. Below us, near at hand, are the minarets, the enclosure walls, the soaring arches and domes of the mosques. They have been a thousand years in the building. We are so high above Ibn-Tulun's mosque we can see not only the minaret with the steps going around the outside but into the great courtyard itself. Down there, too, are the outer walls of Sultan Baybars' congregational mosque.

Previous to Saladin the Fatimid rulers had their palace down on the level, not much above the floodplain of the Nile, but Saladin built his strong point on a spur of the Mokattam Hills overlooking Cairo. He had spent his youth in Syria, where every city had its fortress, and it must, to him, have seemed the most natural thing to build his Citadal where he did. Why, he must have wondered, had the Pharaohs not done the same? The reason was that the Pharaohs ruled over a less strife-ridden country, where people were commanded not

Above, Right. For centuries splendid houses of stone were built in Cairo with little change throughout the Mameluke period and up to the time of Mohammed Ali. A man with cart and horse passes a building with an ornate façade.

so much by force as by tradition and values that were accepted from the top to the bottom of society. It must have been difficult, even to the chivalrous and humane Saladin, to conceive of a society that could be ordered in such a simple way. Yet Saladin's piety led to the introduction into Egypt of theological colleges, the *madrasa* or collegiate mosque, where there were four great porticos in which the four orthodox sects of Islam, the Hanafi, the Shafi'i, the Maliki, and the Hanbali, were taught by learned doctors to the faithful. None of the colleges established by Saladin survive, but others built on the same pattern do, notably Sultan Hasan's at the foot of the Citadel hill, built in 1356-59. This marvelous building, the finest ornate mosque in Cairo—for the austerities of Ibn-Tulun are quite another glory—has nevertheless a soaring and simple exterior reminiscent of ancient temples such as Karnak.

The Mameluke rulers, who ran Egypt from 1250 to the coming of the Ottoman Turks, were slaves. This takes a bit of explaining. There was a practice in the early Middle Ages and in Egypt in particular that led to the importing of young male slaves from Circassia and southern Russia as soldiers who eventually became the rulers. The Arabic word *mamluk* means "belonging to." The greatest of the Mameluke sultans, Baybars, was bought for a few hundred dollars in a Syrian slave market but became, with Saladin, one of the greatest of heroic figures.

Knowing that the Mamelukes were the slave rulers of Egypt, one might cynically surmise that people living under such a regime would be exploited. It would be largely true. These adventurers from the North looked on Egypt and the Egyptians as fair game, but they were not slaves as we understand the term. They were bought in the slave market but they were given special training and privileges which turned them into an elite. A ruler tended to look on his slave officers as his kin rather than his servants, to such a degree that one prince was regarded with suspicion because he had at no time been in servitude. Why one Mameluke ruler was succeeded by another unrelated Mameluke ruler rather than by his son—though exceptionally the Kalaun family hung on father to son for three generations in the thirteenth century—is not entirely clear. There was so little agreement about supreme power in the state that it went to the man backed by the most powerful faction. These Mamelukes were often blue-eyed, fair-haired men who were physically unattractive to the Egyptian or Arab. Even today, the brown-eyed, warm-skinned native of the country looks on blue-eyed or gray-eyed strangers with unease. Blue beads—it would have been the same in ancient Egypt—are used to ward off their evil eye.

The Mamelukes, for all the glory of their architecture and the prosperity that occasionally washed over the country during their rule, probably marked the period when this suppressed social aggression turned into ritual. A personal recollection may illustrate the point. There are some splendid old houses in Cairo, some dating back to the late Middle Ages and still lived in. Tourists can see such a house near the Ibn-Tulun mosque called the Gayer-Anderson house, or Beit Gayer-Anderson, because it was restored by Major Gayer-Anderson and furnished with the appropriate divans, beds, tables, and charcoal burners of the period. From the outside these houses give no hint of the glories inside. The walls are as blank as a factory's and only the doorway will be richly ornamented, though even this is sometimes very simple. The idea is to avoid attracting the envious attention of some powerful man or tax collector. Even when the front door is open all one sees from the street is a blank wall; a passage turns, either this way or that, makes another right-angled turn, and leads one into

Right. The doors, such as these in the main entrance to the House of the Cretans, are often made of small, loosely fitting panels of wood. An ordinary panel would warp in the heat. The pattern is usually elaborate.

Above. Mushrabiya *means "a place for drinking" and is a projecting window made of latticework; inside it porous water jars cool in the current of air that flows down from the roof of the house, where it has been trapped by a north-facing ventilator. It is from the north that the cool wind comes.*

The height of a great reception room, such as this in the House of the Cretans, helps keep the room cool. The richly decorated wooden ceiling is an important feature.

exegesis and doctrine. Great emphasis was placed on memorizing. It was expected that students would know the Koran by heart. They would be taught in groups, in one or another of the many courtyards of the mosque; and certain pillars have become associated with great teachers of the past. There they stood, or more normally sat, with their students in a circle around them. This was the cultural magnet that drew great men from all parts of the Moslem world, such as ibn-Khaldun (1332-1406), who for a time taught at Al Azhar and was the first historian to relate historical development to ordinary physical facts, such as climate and geography; he is among the great historical philosophers on any reckoning. For some years he lived in the Faiyum, where it is pleasant to think of this great man sitting in an arbor near some site where, a thousand years before, the Egyptians had worshipped a crocodile, developing views which the Egyptians would not have understood. They did not understand change and decay in the way that ibn-Khaldun, with the evidence of vanished civilizations before his eyes, was able to formulate. He was the father of historical sociology. It was the magnet of Al Azhar that had drawn him to Egypt. Curious to reflect that this philosopher went from his retreat in the Faiyum, after a short spell as *cadi* in Cairo, on to Damascus, where he met and talked with the terrifying Tamerlane. He was no mere theorist of history.

From the Citadel we can see the Tombs of the Caliphs away to the right where an Egyptian princess was entombed as recently as thirty years ago behind screens of silver lace. The Mamelukes governed Egypt from about 1250 until the coming of the Turks in 1517, and their tombs, less splendid than those of the caliphs, are in the valley to the left together with other and more modest tombs in the so-called City of the Dead, where in sometimes flimsy shanties whole families can be found on certain days with food and drink for the departed—an ancient Egyptian custom indeed.

Over all the sky is cloudless and empty. Even in this great metropolitan center much of what the eye sees is sky. In the Delta one looks from the green fields of cotton and clover to the white dome over some departed saint or sheikh and then to the great emptiness of sky, blue, clear, and fleckless in the early morning, painfully luminous and yet drained at the height of day, then pink and golden toward evening, when the air has that much more dust in it because of the movement of men, animals, machines, and the rising currents of warm air. The sky lacks the drama of European or American clouds. It does not make statements. It is remote. The scavenging kites that once circled over European cities are still to be seen in Cairo swooping to snatch bread from a balcony. They are less common than they were even a few years ago but they are all that stir in the sky. They alone catch the eye and one walks through countryside and town feeling on the skin of things. Perhaps this was why the Turks like very tall pencil minarets on their mosques. As the spires of Gothic cathedrals probe the sky, so do the soaring columns we see here and there marking some holy building that went up after the Turks came in 1517. The most notable of these Turkish minarets are at the Citadel itself, where Mohammed Ali at the beginning of the nineteenth century built his opulent mosque, the most obviously eye-catching place in modern Cairo. The pinnacles catch the morning sun as it comes up behind the Mokattam Hills before any mosque, *madrasa*, *khan* (the old caravanserai where travelers lodged), or even tall modern office block in the city down below.

The city that we see from this vantage point under the Mokattam Hills is the medieval city of Cairo. At roughly the same time as the *madrasa* of Sultan Hasan was being built, The *Thousand and One*

Nights was being assembled and put in the form this marvelous collection now has. So extensive was the rewriting of these tales, many of which were Egyptian but many of which, too, had their origin in other parts of the Near East and in India, that it can be taken as an expression of the values of the society that flourished in this city over 500 years ago. In spite of Baghdad and Haroun-al-Raschid, if there is one city of the *Arabian Nights* that city is Cairo.

This is not to say the stories were created there under the Mamelukes. Some were. The Cairo tales are usually about thieving, roguery, or what the Elizabethans called coney-catching. It was the nearest the popular entertainers of the time came to dissidence. A society where justice was arbitrary naturally chose villains as its heroes, and the stories about them catch something of the jeering, punning humor of the Egyptians of today. But most of these tales come from other lands. Some are very ancient but they have all been filtered through the medieval Arabic of the city, and through the temperament of the Egyptians of the time. They were stories for telling, not reading. To make the stories more vivid for his listeners, the *sha'er*, or storyteller, who broke up his narrative by notes on a single-stringed viol, would bring in local color, local references, and an appeal to the circumstances in which they lived. In their way they expressed something of the times in which they were spoken, as, say, the plays of Shakespeare tell us about the Elizabethans. When Herodotus was in Egypt two thousand years before, he heard tales about the way tombs were robbed and Pyramids built which exhibit the same naïve wonder as in the *Arabian Nights*.

The stories are a repository of medieval superstition, some of it still current. One of the oddities of religious belief is that whereas the Moslem, the Christian, and the Jew, to name the adherents of the three great monotheistic faiths in Egypt, held firmly to their respective doctrines, they seemed quite ready to accept each other's superstitions. In Egypt, Moslem, Christian, and Jew all believed in powerful and evil spirits: the jinn, for example, who have existed on earth since before men were created; afreets, who were malevolent ghosts; and ghouls, who were scavengers. Edward Lane, the Englishman who lived in Egypt from 1825 to 1849 and translated the *Thousand and One Nights*, also wrote a classic study of the society in which he found himself, *Manners and Customs of the Modern Egyptians* (1836)—"the most perfect picture of a people's life that has ever been written," as one friendly critic described it—frequently referring to the *Nights* to clarify some point he was making about the beliefs or habits of the Cairenes of his time, as that a date stone, for example, cast casually to the ground might kill a jinn, or that birds and beasts have a language of their own.

For all the piety of *Alf Leyleh wa-Layh* (the *Nights*)—each story begins and ends with blessings on the Prophet—the real god of the collection is chance. Only through chance can the oppressed prosper. Perhaps, in opening a fish he has caught, a great diamond is found inside and this is the basis of the finder's prosperity. They are not ethical stories. Virtue, hard work, honesty, and truthfulness are desirable in themselves, but they do not lead to success. Time and chance, as the writer of Ecclesiastes wrote, happeneth to all men. This fundamental skepticism about the values of this life which the *Arabian Nights* conveys tells us more about the medieval Egyptian and his resignation to the will of others than any formal study of the theology of that time.

The two largest rooms in a medieval kind of house are the mandara *(right), which, traditionally, was where men were received; and the* ka'ah *(left), a lofty room on the first floor, as in the House of the Cretans.*

First Overleaf. Old houses, like the Sihaymi, are built to a pattern around a courtyard, and the reception rooms are lofty, with alcoves and wooden grilles for coolness. The colored-glass windows, usually with abstract or flower designs, are quite high in the room, sometimes at the top of the lattice windows. They are known as kamariyahs. *The grotesque design at right is quite unusual. The individual pieces of glass are bedded in plaster and the whole is held in a wooden frame.*

Second Overleaf. On the outcrop of rock to the east of Cairo, Saladin, the great leader of Islam during the Crusades, built his Citadel, or fortress, to command the whole country of Egypt. On this site Mohammed Ali began in 1824 his great mosque in the Turkish style, modeled on the Nuri Osmaniyeh mosque at Constantinople. It was completed by his son, Said Pasha. With its tall, pencil minarets it forms the most striking landmark in Cairo.

The Land of Egypt

Egypt is 800 miles long and, at Kalabsha, narrows to 170 yards wide. South of Cairo the widest extent of the irrigated area is only thirteen miles. The Delta is different and, from the most ancient times, was recognized as being different. This fertile area nowadays grows cotton, rice, and vegetables, and is broken up by irrigation canals, shallow lakes, and salt beds. In Pharaonic times there were marshes where the papyrus grew. It grows there no longer, though the marshes remain, the haunt of duck and plover. To find the plant that, more than any other, made Egyptian civilization possible, and European civilization, too, one has to go into Nubia. Nowadays, where the papyrus grew and Moses was reputedly discovered in the bulrushes, there are fields of *berseem* (a kind of clover) and cotton, all painted on the flat earth as though by poster artists. Along the raised tracks at the side of the canals trot the silver asses with a pannier on each flank. There are lines of palm trees, casuarinas, and—a recent importation—eucalyptus for shade. In the mud-brick houses there is a mud-brick stove on top of which the family sleeps on cold nights. Flat unleavened bread is baked here and eaten with cheese, onions, roast chicken, eggs, and fish (rarely meat) to keep body and soul together, as the peasant would undoubtedly put it.

In the Thebaid the cultivated black land extends between desert and desert. Fields of barley, maize, wheat, and sugarcane fill the flat land between one ruined temple and the next. The Coptic church or monastery with its cross slightly askew is loud with clocks. They are important because time is important in the Coptic liturgy; and the cock, the hens, and the occasional goat that wander in and out of the sacred enclosure are as welcome as they would have been to the ancient forebears of the present Egyptians. Every living thing is some aspect of the truth—not mankind only but animals as well, who in their innocence and self-preoccupation speak eloquently of what it is to be flesh. A truth about human beings should have equal application to the ass, the camel, the buffalo, and the white ibis in the fields. There is not—and this is the special Egyptian reservation about Islam and Christianity—one destiny for humankind and another for the animals.

Most of Egypt is desert. In the east are the mountains of the Arabian or Eastern Desert, which gave gold and copper. On the other side of the Red Sea is Sinai and the place where Moses received, over 8,000 feet above sea level, the Ten Commandments. To the west is the greatest of Egyptian oases, the Faiyum, where the land is undulating and, because the water level is below that of the Nile, waterwheels are to be heard groaning in sorrow. Here grow grapes, prickly pears, guavas, mangoes, eggplants, and artichokes. Further west are other oases. The rest is sand, vast enough to swallow armies. At least one army, that of the Persian Cambyses, disappeared without trace in 524 B.C. but may yet be found with its baggage train, if the wind shifts, preserved in some arid ditch.

One tends to forget the length of the medieval trade routes and the immense journeys men were capable of taking at no greater speed than that of the horse or of sail. The Arab ibn-Batuta traveled from Tunis to Cairo and on through India to China between 1340 and 1350 A.D., eventually to return and write a book about his travels. China was a source of silk to the Romans. Such was the trade with India in the late Middle Ages that the discovery of the Cape route by the Portuguese hurt the Egyptian economy, which was already in a bad way because of maladministration. The last independent

Modern Egypt in the Making

Left. Ismailia on Lake Timsah, halfway along the Suez Canal, was created when the Canal was built and together with Port Fuad in the north and Port Tewfik in the south was a pleasant place for pilots and other Canal people to live. It was severely damaged in the conflict with Israel but is being reconstructed.

Overleaf. The great dunes of the Western Desert, like this one near Kharga, remind us what the land would be like without the Nile. Sand rather than water makes Egypt an island.

There is no doubt at all that for the ordinary man Egypt was a hard place to live in during the seventeenth and eighteenth centuries. The administration of the country was so corrupt and justice so arbitrary that the peasant or trader had no motive but to provide a bare standard of living, for anything more would have been creamed off by the Bey or the tax collector. Fertile areas went out of cultivation, particularly in the Delta, where the cultivated land shrank by a third. The Faiyum became more or less depopulated because of Bedouin raids, the population of the cities declined—that of Alexandria to something like 4,000—and travelers from Europe (usually on the way to India) found a general feeling of helplessness among the people, who appeared never to question the right of foreigners to rule over them; they were defenseless against brutality and it was by no means uncommon for a village to be completely evacuated when troops were seen in the vicinity. Troops were maintained throughout the provinces to collect taxes, usually by force. If caught, village honor demanded that the fellah paid nothing until he had been beaten, and the longer he lasted before producing his few wretched coins, the greater the honor.

Some years ago one of the richer Bedouin families who had made a success of camel breeding sent a son to be educated in Cairo. He was asked why this extraordinary gesture had been made, for the Bedouins are traditionally suspicious of life in the city and would go there only for some specific deal, returning to the desert as quickly as possible. The boy said he had an ancestor who was not an Arab but a fellah from the Nile Valley. This made the tribe more tolerant of Egyptian ways. Why did he have such an ancestor? It seems that there was once, perhaps a hundred and fifty, two hundred, two hundred and fifty years ago, an *omdah*, or headman, who kept his money in a sack at the bottom of a canal. The sack was at one end of a rope. The other end was pegged into the ground and masked by vegetation. When, as inevitably happened, troops arrived and found this rope they asked the *omdah*, his being the nearest house, what was at the end of it. He said he knew nothing of the rope, he had not seen it before, but it was the custom in those parts for live fish to be kept in submerged sacks so that when they were wanted for food they would be quite fresh. Sure enough, and much to his amazement, when the sack was drawn up from the bottom of the canal it did indeed contain nothing but a live fish and the *omdah* knew that someone in the village had robbed him and that there was nothing he could do about it. One of his sons had been so offended at this lack of honor among the fellaheen that he had gone into the desert with two goats and become the guest of a Bedouin family, into which he soon married. "You see," said the scholar Bedouin, "there is honor in the desert." The story illustrates the contempt of the Bedouins for a settled way of life, the long folk memory they possess, and the way tax-gathering soldiers behaved long ago.

The greatest event in modern Egypt was the arrival of Napoleon Bonaparte in 1798. He had managed to persuade the Directory in Paris that this would be the best way of destroying British influence in the Mediterranean and recovering India, which, like Alexander before him, worked powerfully on his imagination. The importance of the occasion was not so much military as scholarly. With him he took scientists of all kinds, geologists, botanists, historians, engineers, and surveyors, with the idea of recording and assessing the resources of the country. It was a remarkably farsighted thing to do. Having defeated the Mamelukes at the Battle of the Pyramids—after making

213

Above. Between the Mediterranean and the Qattara Depression, which is below sea level, is a neck of the Western Desert along which invaders in all periods have come. A railway track follows the coast from Alexandria to Libya but not many trains run these days.
Upper Right. Old tanks litter the Egyptian deserts. This one is just east of the Suez Canal, in Sinai.
Lower Right. Flat-topped carts, pulled by donkeys—the animals most essential to Egypt's well-being—trundle along a road kept specially for them at Mezghuna.

Top. Aerial acrobatics over
the Nile at Cairo. The modern
city has crowded down toward
the Nile, and once the exclusive
place to live was on the great
island of Gezireh, with its
Sporting Club and luxury
apartments. Medieval Cairo kept
away from the Nile.
Above. The Citadel was built
by Saladin, the great leader
of Islam during the Crusades.
Its ramparts are the best place
to view the city.

Above. So many people throng through central Cairo that in the Midan el Tahrir (Liberation Square) raised pedestrian ways have been built to cope with the press of human beings. The Egyptian Museum is in the distance and, at left, a Hilton hotel where once a Turkish barracks stood.

Left. Egypt is a socialist republic but until recently under military control. Of late a liberalization has led to a revival of parliamentary institutions.

Suez and the Wider World

The Suez Canal was opened in 1869 by a flotilla led by L'Aigle, *carrying, among others, the Empress Eugénie of France. The nationalization of the Canal by Egypt in 1956 prompted the Anglo-French assault on the Canal Zone.*

The Suez Canal was opened in 1869 but it was not the first occasion when boats were able to sail from the Mediterranean to the Red Sea. Sesostris was given the credit for building the first link through the Wadi Tumulat from the Nile to the Red Sea although in fact the first effective canal, linking the Nile to the Gulf of Suez, was begun by Necho and completed by Darius. De Lesseps, who built the Suez Canal, was not even the first man to conceive the idea of running a canal through the isthmus, for Haroun-al-Raschid (of the *Thousand and One Nights*) entertained the idea in the eighth century A.D. To Napoleon a thousand years later it was an obvious thing to do. He ordered a survey but his engineers reported, wrongly as it turned out, a difference in level of twenty-nine feet between the Red Sea and the Mediterranean. This would have caused any canal to run like a river. There is, in fact, an actual difference but it is so slight that the gentle movement of water between the Red Sea (which is infinitesimally higher) and the Mediterranean is scarcely discernible.

It was the building of the Suez Canal by an internationally financed company (mainly French) that put Egypt on the main road between Europe and the East. Port Said became a new town where the steamers recoaled and the passengers went ashore to shop in the great emporium of Simon Artz. It was a Levantine, rather than an Egyptian, town where, in the course of time, a considerable population of Greeks and Italians established themselves. To the east the Italian or French Suez Canal pilot would see the salt stretches where once the ancient city of Pelusium had been. And to the west, the brackish salt water of Lake Manzala, where prawns of an enormous size were caught and fishermen, as they pulled in their nets, could see, down below in the water, the columns and stone fragments of remotely ancient, Ptolemaic and Roman cities.

The Suez Canal came into existence because of the personal friendship between a French engineer and the ruler of Egypt, Said Pasha. The French engineer was Ferdinand de Lesseps, who had a special attitude toward canal building. He belonged to a group of French intellectuals who believed—contrary to the best scientific opinion of the time—that there was no significant difference of level between the Mediterranean and the Red Sea. What is more, they believed that the building of canals, in Suez and Panama for example, would lead to such benefits it would be no exaggeration to say it would bring about a regeneration of mankind. On such waters of theory are practical measures sometimes floated. De Lesseps raised the money by opening subscriptions for the Suez Canal Company. The first spade of sand was turned, near the present Port Said (which did not, of course, exist at that time), April 25, 1859, and the Canal was triumphantly opened ten years later, in November 1869, with a flotilla of boats passing from the Mediterranean to the Red Sea, led by the *Aigle* with the French Empress Eugénie on board. It became clear to all concerned that whatever benefits to mankind the Canal might confer, at least one thing was evident: the Red Sea was not significantly higher than the Mediterranean.

The Canal was built by the same people who built the Pyramids but without the same religious enthusiasm, one suspects. To begin with, the labor was forced, and although the pay and conditions were possibly better than the men normally expected, European opinion, particularly in England, was such that the corvée was abandoned and more modern means of excavation—machines, for example—were introduced. This, more than any other factor, led to the success of the enterprise. It is not always true that liberal values lead to the betterment of the human condition or the successful conclusion of enterprises, but it does seem to have happened in Suez. The British in particular thought the Canal technically impossible. When they also decided that it was morally reprehensible, their opposition to the scheme was fortified. No country, however, stood to gain more from the Suez Canal—Egypt apart—than the United Kingdom, because of its interests in India. When the Egyptian Government nationalized the Suez Canal Company in 1956 there was general expectation that the Egyptian Suez Canal pilots would be unable to get the boats through the Canal without disaster. Most of the pilots were Europeans and they had been removed. The Egyptians did, however, get the boats through successfully, as no one who knew anything about the Canal or the Egyptians ever doubted they would.

The British were the real power in the land from 1882 until the end of World War II in 1946, when the British military presence was reduced to the Canal Zone, and 1955, when a final evacuation took place. In 1952 King Farouk had embarked at Alexandria after being driven from his throne by the army which, much as Great Britain and France might regret it, represented a genuine national movement. The Anglo-French attack on the Canal Zone in 1956, ostensibly to separate the Egyptian and Israeli forces, appears in the perspective of history to have been a miscalculation. It is characteristic of the Egyptian people that they should have seen this attack, like the British naval bombardment of Alexandria in 1882, as a regrettable European failure to understand the complex currents that were beginning to flow in Egypt; and, after a flirtation with Soviet Russia and the kind of industrial and economic aid the Soviets could provide—notably in the building of the new Aswan Dam and the creation of Lake Nasser in Upper Egypt—the present mood of the Egyptian people seems to be for better understanding with the Western powers of Europe and the United States. Even Israel seems to loom less important in Egyptian thinking than the economic problems that face the country. The greatest is the pressure of population on natural resources. As recently as 1946 the population was 18 million and the population of Cairo 2 million. In 1977 the population was over 30 million. Cairo is one of the most populous cities of the world. Nine million people live there, roughly the number of people who live in the Greater London area or in the city of New York. By the end of the century the population of Egypt is expected to approach 80 million. The geographical area of the country is 400,000 square miles, which is slightly smaller than the states of California, Oregon, Washington, and Nevada put together. But only one square mile out of fifteen is habitable (except by the Bedouins). No doubt a rising standard of living and education will lead to a slackening of the birth rate but this pressure of population on resources is the greatest problem the country has to face.

Right. The Gulf of Suez at night. These ships are lined up waiting to pass through the Canal. Traffic can be channeled in either direction at this strategically important area. Overleaf. Anglo-French intervention resulted in part from the fear that Egypt would take an unwarrantable control of east-west communication. The war between Israel and Egypt and the desire to separate the combatants was another important factor.

although the natural wells and springs have been exploited since antiquity, it is only very recently that the real wealth of water was discovered, by accident almost, for it was a by-product of drilling for oil. There is no oil.

Once ways have been found of bringing this water to the surface and using it for irrigation without its evaporation leading to a salination of the soil, there is obviously room for a considerable increase of agriculture. The energy for raising the water will presumably come from electricity generated at the new Aswan Dam two or three hundred miles away, but salination is a bigger problem.

The uplands and crags of the Western Desert will, however, never respond to the attention of any scientific team. The particular quality of these uplands is the intolerable blaze of heat in the summer noon, the austere silence at a time of no wind in a land that is nakedly geological and meteorological. There is no rain—no rain whatsoever, except on some freakish occasion when a sudden storm springs up, the *wadis* run with water, and miraculously in its wake desert plants and flowers spring from the hibernated seed. Travelers report the remains of fossilized trees. They must have grown when the fossil water was laid down a million years ago. Since that time, the sun, winter cold, and the wind have scrubbed hard at this limestone and left it dramatic and uncompromising. Let us not be deceived by the promise of underground water. The oases are there on sufferance.

The Egyptians are capable of surprising the world again as they surprised it in antiquity. One thing is certain—they are a special kind of people. The peculiarities of their geography and history mark them out from the inhabitants of any other country one can think of; some of their greatest differences in character and temperament are with their neighbors in the Arab world and in Israel. Basically the Egyptians want to be left alone. They have been at the receiving end of ideological and religious thrusts for far too long. If their internal economic problems can be solved—and the greatest of these is population growth—Egypt will no doubt be playing a greater part in the world and in a way that is appropriate for a people with such roots.

The vitality of any country is dependent in great measure on the beliefs it has about the significance of life and the legitimate objectives for which human beings can strive. In the past these have had a religious foundation in Egypt. What happens when and if the old faiths wither? Egypt is now officially a socialist republic. Will it make the transition from a society oriented toward God to one with values that make man himself the measure? It remains to be seen whether socialism will provide the vision that will take the country into the next century with security, a higher standard of living, and social harmony. Social harmony yes, for that is the sort of people the Egyptians are; but a larger sense of purpose may prove elusive. There is a poem by G. K. Chesterton that speaks of the English people who "have not spoken yet." Whether or not the English have been inarticulate about their deep Englishness is a matter on which more than one view is possible. But the poem really does apply to the Egyptians. They have not spoken for a long, long time. When they do, will it be because they are looking at the rest of the world; or will they be more inward-looking and, in Voltaire's words, seek simply to cultivate their own gardens in the traditional Egyptian way? We shall have to wait and see. An old country is struggling to be born.

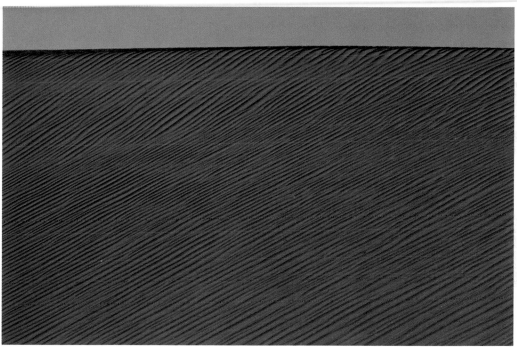

*Left. The dunes are not as great
as they are farther west—in the
Great Sand Sea, for example—
but they are large enough to
swallow a convoy in a storm.
Farther north, a Persian army
disappeared leaving no trace,
while marching toward Siwa.
Above, Overleaf. Ridges indicate
the direction of the prevailing
winds. In summer a hot wind
blows from the south to the west.
Sand spouts form, sucking sand
thousands of feet into the air.
This is* khamseen *time when the
Nile Valley gets suffocating
dust-laden storms.
But the austerities of rock and
sand have a beauty of their own.*

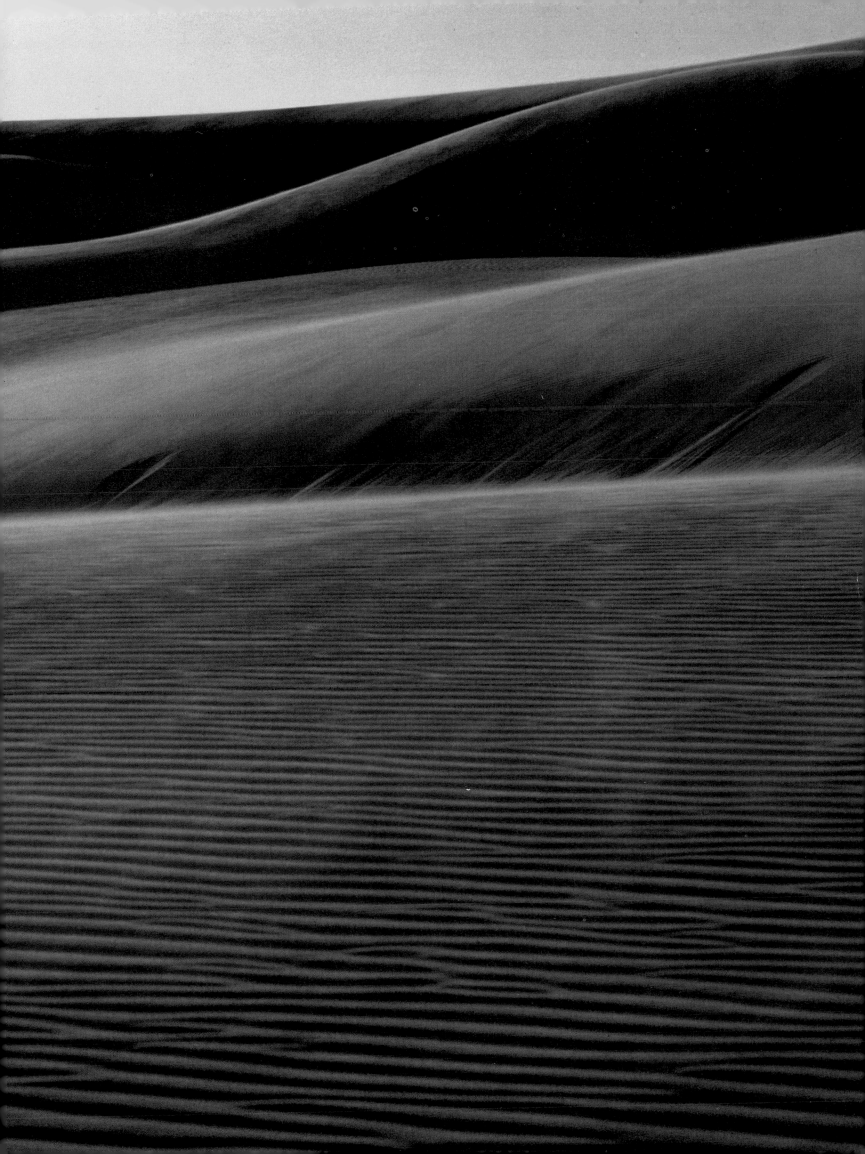

Chronology

This chart lists the major periods and rulers of Egypt from ancient times to the present. The individuals included are chosen from those rulers most significant in the course of Egyptian history and those whom the author has singled out as of most importance to Egyptian culture. The dates of the earliest epochs and kings are approximate and, may be revised in the light of new research. To further complicate matters periods of unrest in ancient times permitted the rise of weak rival dynasties whose competing claims lead to overlapping dates.

For the Islamic and modern Egyptian period the table lists the major categories of rulers, e.g. caliphs, in the first column, dynasties of governors in the second column and individuals in the third column. The names of governors are printed in italics whereas the names of kings, sultans, modern leaders are in roman type.

Since its conquest in the seventh century A.D. by followers of Mohammed, Egypt has been ruled by a succession of dynasties including Umayyads, Abbasids, Tulunids, Fatimids, Ayyubids, Mamelukes, Ottomans, Khedives, some of whom produced outstanding leaders, such as Ahmad Ibn-Tulun, Saladin, Baybars, and Mohammed Ali. Thus, from the time of the Pharoah in the third century B.C., Egypt has not had a native ruler until an upheaval in 1952 brought Gamal Abdel Nasser power.

Periods	Dynasties	Rulers
EARLY DYNASTIES (ca. 3100-2686 B.C.)	DYNASTY 1 (ca. 3100-2890 B.C.)	Narmer (Menes?)
	DYNASTY 2 (ca. 2890-2686 B.C.)	
OLD KINGDOM (2686-2160 B.C.)	DYNASTY 3 (ca. 2686-2613 B.C.)	Zoser (ca. 19 years)
	DYNASTY 4 (ca. 2613-2494 B.C.)	Snefru (ca. 19 years) Cheops (ca. 23 years) Chephren (ca. 25 years) Mycerinus (ca. 28 years)
	DYNASTY 5 (ca. 2494-2345 B.C.)	
	DYNASTY 6 (ca. 2345-2181 B.C.)	Pepy II (ca. 94 years)
FIRST INTERMEDIATE PERIOD (ca. 2181-2133 B.C.)	DYNASTY 7 (ca. 2181-2173 B.C.)	
	DYNASTY 8 (ca. 2173-2160 B.C.)	
	DYNASTIES 9 and 10 (ca. 2160-2133 B.C.)	
MIDDLE KINGDOM (ca. 2133-1633 B.C.)	DYNASTY 11 (ca. 2133-1991 B.C.)	Mentuhotep II (2060-2010 B.C.)
	DYNASTY 12 (ca. 1991-1786 B.C.)	Sesostris I (1971-1928 B.C.) Sesostris III (1878-1843 B.C.) Amenemmes III (1842-1797 B.C.)
SECOND INTERMEDIATE PERIOD (ca. 1786-1544)	DYNASTY 13 (ca. 1786-1633 B.C.)	
	DYNASTY 14 (ca. 1633-1603 B.C.)	
	DYNASTIES 15 and 16 (ca. 1603-1650 B.C.) (The Hyksos)	
	DYNASTY 17 (ca. 1650-1544 B.C.)	
NEW KINGDOM (ca. 1558-1085 B.C.)	DYNASTY 18 (ca. 1558-1303 B.C.)	Amenophis I (1533-1512 B.C.) Thutmose I (1512-1500 B.C.) Thutmose II (1500-1490 B.C.) Queen Hatshepsut (1490-1469 B.C.) Thutmose III (1490-1436 B.C.)

Periods	Dynasties	Rulers
		Amenophis II (1438-1412 B.C.) Thutmose IV (1412-1402 B.C.) Amenophis III (1402-1365 B.C.) Akhenaton (1365-1349 B.C.) Smenkhkare (1349-1347 B.C.) Tutankhamun (1347-1338 B.C. or 1334-1325 B.C.)
	DYNASTY 19 (ca. 1303-1200 B.C.)	Ramses I (1303-1301 B.C.) Seti I (1301-1290 B.C.) Ramses II (1290-1224 B.C.) Merneptah (1224-1214 B.C.)
	DYNASTY 20 (ca. 1200-1085 B.C.)	Ramses III (1198-1166 B.C.)
THIRD INTERMEDIATE PERIOD (1085-656 B.C.)	DYNASTY 21 (ca. 1085-945 B.C.)	
	DYNASTY 22 (ca. 945-717 B.C.)	
	DYNASTY 23 (ca. 817-730 B.C.)	
	DYNASTY 24 (ca. 730-715 B.C.)	
	DYNASTY 25 (ca. 715-656 B.C.)	
SAITE RENAISSANCE (664-525 B.C.)	DYNASTY 26 (664-525 B.C.)	Psamtik (664-610 B.C.) Necho (609-594 B.C.)
LATE DYNASTIES (525-330 B.C.)	DYNASTY 27 (FIRST PERSIAN DOMINATION—525-404 B.C.)	Darius I (522-485 B.C.)
	DYNASTY 28 (404-398 B.C.)	
	DYNASTY 29 (398-378 B.C.)	
	DYNASTY 30 (378-341 B.C.)	Nekhthorheb II (Nectanebo II) (359-341 B.C.)
	DYNASTY 31 (SECOND PERSIAN DOMINATION—341-330 B.C.)	Darius III (335-330 B.C.)

Periods	Dynasties	Rulers
MACEDONIAN DOMINATION (332-304 B.C.)		Alexander the Great (332-323 B.C.)
PTOLEMAIC DYNASTY (304-30 B.C.)		Ptolemy I (305-285 B.C.) Cleopatra VII (51-49, 48-30 B.C.)
ROMAN EMPERORS (30 B.C.-A.D. 642)		Augustus (27 B.C.-14 A.D.) Diocletian (284-305)
ORTHODOX CALIPHS (632-661)		
UMAYYAD CALIPHS (661-750)		Abd-al-Malik (685-705) Walid (705-715)
ABBASID CALIPHS (750-969)		Haroun al-Raschid (786-809) Mamun (813-833)
	Tulunids *(868-905)*	*Ahmad Ibn-Tulun* *(868-883)*
	Ikshidids *(935-969)*	*Mohammah Ikhshid* *(935-946)*
FATIMID CALIPHS (909-1171)		al-Hakim (966-1020) Mustansir (1035-1094) Amir (1101-1130)
AYYUBIDS (1169-1250)		Saladin (1169-1193) Kamil (1218-1238)
MAMELUKE SULTANS (1252-1517)		Baybars (1260-1277) Hasan (1347-1354, 1354-1361) Barkuk (1382-1389, 1390-1398)
OTTOMANS (1517-1798)		
FRENCH OCCUPATION (1798-1805)		
KHEDIVES (1805-1882)		Mohammed Ali (1805-1848) Ishmail (1863-1882)

Periods	Dynasties	Rulers
BRITISH OCCUPATION (1882-1922)		Husayn Kamil (1914-1917) Ahmad Fuad (1917-1922)
KINGDOM OF EGYPT (1922-1952)		King Fuad I (1922-1936) King Farouk (1936-1952)
REPUBLIC OF EGYPT (1952-)		Gamal Abdel Nasser (1952-1970) Anwar el-Sadat (1970-)

*For the photographs in this book the Leicaflex SL2 MOT and Leica M
cameras were used with their lens systems, including a 15mm f8
Hologon on a Leica M3. A tripod was used at all times.*

*Nearly all of the photographs were taken with existing light on
Kodachrome and Ektachrome film.*

Prepared and Produced by Chanticleer Press:
Publisher: Paul Steiner
Editor-in-Chief: Milton Rugoff
Managing Editor: Gudrun Buettner
Project Editor: Susan Costello
Editorial Assistants: Mary Beth Brewer, Richard Christopher
Production: Helga Lose, Ray Patient
Art Associates: Carol Nehring, Dolores Santoliquido, Johann Wechter
Design: Massimo Vignelli